CALVIN FOR EVERYONE
INSTITUTES OF THE CHRISTIAN RELIGION
IN MODERN ENGLISH

CALVIN FOR EVERYONE
INSTITUTES OF THE CHRISTIAN RELIGION
IN MODERN ENGLISH

BOOK I: THE KNOWLEDGE OF GOD
THE CREATOR

John Calvin
Paraphrased and Edited by Caroline Weerstra

Common Life Press
Schenectady, New York

Cover design by Leah Min Trouwborst.

This paraphrased and abridged edition of John Calvin's *Institutes of the Christian Religion: The Knowledge of God the Creator* is based primarily on the English translation produced by Henry Beveridge in 1845.

Scripture taken from the New King James Version. Copyright © 1982 by Thomas Nelson, Inc. Used by permission. All rights reserved.

To Danielle
because she wanted to read Calvin

CONTENTS

ACKNOWLEDGMENTS

I am deeply grateful for the work of Henry Beveridge, whose 1845 translation of John Calvin's *Institutes of the Christian Religion* formed the basis of this paraphrased edition.

I must also express my gratitude for the work of Ford Lewis Battles, whose footnotes in the 1960 translation of the *Institutes* provided me with a direction of study in my own quest to better understand Calvin.

I am indebted to Greg Bahnsen's lectures on the *Institutes*, and to my own pastor Tom Trouwborst for providing the tapes of those lectures and explaining them to me.

I would also like to thank Ruben Zartman for kindly undertaking the tedious task of editing this book.

Finally, many thanks to my husband Rick for his love and encouragement throughout the writing of this book and always.

INTRODUCTION

The Westminster Confession of Faith calls us to translate the Bible into the "vulgar language of every nation." In this sense, Caroline Weerstra has written a *vulgar* book. When Christian parents hear or see something vulgar, they often frantically flip channels or snatch away a magazine. When you read this book, you should call your children into the den. Sit them down, pull out their earphones, and read them this book.

The words in this book are from Calvin's *Institutes*. God used John Calvin's *Institutes of the Christian Religion* to change the world. Martin Luther officially started the party we call the Reformation. But Calvin's unforgettable logic and clarity *immortalized* the party. Calvin presents in his *Institutes* a holistic vision of the gospel-infused (c)atholic church. He transformed nations, churches, and, most importantly, the hearts of many. Some have called Calvin the founder of America. Is that going too far? Perhaps. Regardless, if Mr. Calvin never penned the Institutes, we would have a different nation today. Calvin helped define the West as we know it.

Christ reformed an *elitist* Judaism. He consorted with tax collectors, sinners, the poor, the sick, and the blind. The Reformation dealt with an *elitist* Catholicism. Reformers brought the healing words of Christ to the rabble, the downtrodden, and the down-and-out. While not denying the separate calling of the clergy, the Reformers emphasized that every believer, through Christ, is a prophet, priest and king. The Temple curtain has been torn in two. Through Christ, we now have access to God and His Word, regardless of how we scored in standardized testing.

In that sense, this book is vulgar, meaning that it is in the common language. Not crude like some TV shows or music lyrics in this modern age. I use this term because this book "belongs to the masses." Caroline has presented Calvin's genius in the modern American language. Calvin was a 16th century scholar. He used big words. He used archaic words. Caroline has made Calvin eminently readable while retaining his content.

We should not be ashamed of expressing the gospel in the common language. Christ's life was "of the masses." He died on the cross in a manner of execution reserved for the lowest and vilest of humanity. He came down to us. Way down. And the salvation He promises is for the common folk. It makes fools of the wise men and wise men of the foolish. It is the faith of infants and little children, of the crippled and wounded. Christianity makes the common look glorious. This book is gloriously for the common folk.

I earnestly pray that through Caroline's efforts, Calvin would be taken to the street. God used Calvin to change the world. God still uses him to change hearts today.

Pastor Thomas Trouwborst
Calvary Orthodox Presbyterian Church
Schenectady, New York

CHAPTER 1
KNOWING GOD AND OURSELVES

Unless We Know Ourselves, We Cannot Know God

History Corner

John Calvin wrote five Latin editions of the *Institutes* during his lifetime. He also translated his book into French (his native language).

Calvin's final Latin edition, published in 1559, serves as the base manuscript for most modern translations.

The first English translation of the *Institutes* was completed by Thomas Norton in 1561, three years before Calvin's death. Norton was the son-in-law of Thomas Cranmer, a leader of the English Reformation.

Almost everything that we know (or at least everything true and worth knowing) can be divided into two main ideas: the knowledge of God and the knowledge of ourselves. These are not two completely separate concepts; they are so closely tied together that it is difficult to decide which comes first.

Anyone who begins to seriously consider himself must soon turn to thinking about God, because it is in God that we all live and move.[1] Humans are remarkable creatures with wonderful abilities. Clearly, these abilities are gifts from God, since everything we have comes from God. The generous benefits which God bestows on us are like tiny dewdrops from heaven, reminding us that He is the source of all good things.

However, it is not solely in our abilities that we catch a glimpse of our Creator. When we see our poverty and neediness, then we look toward heaven for comfort. In our hunger, we search for something which will satisfy us. In our fear, we learn to be humble and to acknowledge that we are not self-sufficient. As we recognize our own shortcomings — how little we understand, how much we lack, and especially how corrupt and evil our own hearts are—we realize that all true wisdom, all real goodness, everything pure and right is found in God alone.

---

[1] Acts 17:28

Which came first, the chicken or the egg?

Calvin opens the *Institutes* by setting up a dilemma of circular causes: *A causes B, but B is also necessary for A, so which is the ultimate cause?* Calvin lays out this puzzle: our knowledge of our sinful condition causes us to seek God, but we must know something of God in order to understand our depravity. How can we determine which comes first?

Calvin's goal is not to solve this dilemma. Instead, he uses this puzzle to set the foundation for a more important concept which will carry through the rest of the book: our existence is in every way dependent upon God. Even the knowledge of ourselves is inextricably bound together with the knowledge of God, so much so that we cannot even fully separate these categories.

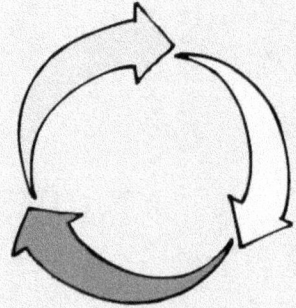

As we seek God, we become increasingly discontent with ourselves. If we were satisfied with our current condition, we would never perceive the necessity of changing. This sense of our own incompleteness propels us forward. The knowledge of ourselves not only awakens us to our need of God, but also leads us by the hand to find Him.

Without Knowing God, We Cannot Know Ourselves

We have established the necessity of having a true understanding of ourselves and our desperate condition in order to know God; we will never search for Him unless we understand our need. However, we should also recognize the converse: we must know God in order to understand ourselves.

Human pride blinds us to our real condition. We are far too quick to judge ourselves to be "good" people—and not only good, but also very intelligent and perceptive and skilled decision-makers. If we merely compare ourselves to other people, then we may maintain this idiotic self-assurance indefinitely. Everyone and everything in this world has been contaminated by evil. Thus, it is easy to find someone to whom we may compare ourselves and say, "I am a much better person."

Of course, all of this self-congratulation is silliness and hypocrisy. We are like people who have been staring so long at dirt and grime that anything even slightly less filthy appears brilliantly clean. We are our own greatest flatterers, and so we imagine that we are doing very well.

When we raise our thoughts above ourselves and look toward God, our smug attitude crumbles. When we consider His holiness and His wisdom, we recognize the pitiful inadequacy of our own efforts. We may have once thought of ourselves as strong, but we must conclude that we are weak, wicked, and foolish creatures. Our fantasy that we are "clean" collapses when our shabby righteousness is contrasted to the perfect purity of God.

Mankind Confronted With God's Majesty

Scripture gives many examples of people who were stricken with terror and wonder when they drew near to God. Even strong and steadfast men were shaken by the glory of God to the point that they feared they would be destroyed. We must conclude from these stories that people are never so acutely aware of their own sinfulness as when they are forced to compare themselves to God's majesty.

The Bible tells us about many occasions when people became so panic-stricken in the presence of God that they cried out, "We will die, because the Lord has appeared to us!"[1] The story of Job reveals God's wisdom, power, and holiness in such a way that all who read it must acknowledge their own stupidity, weakness, and sinfulness. Abraham, as he drew near to God's glory, realized that he was only dust.[2] Elijah had to wrap his mantle around his face as God approached.[3] Isaiah said, "Then the moon will be disgraced and the sun ashamed; for the LORD of hosts will reign."[4] Even the sun and moon—the brightest objects we have ever seen—are like darkness compared to the glory of God.

We see that the knowledge of God and the knowledge of ourselves are closely tied together. The knowledge of God brings forth a better understanding of ourselves, and a true understanding of ourselves compels us to seek more of God. We will consider both of these more fully. Since God should be first in all things, we will begin by studying God.

---

[1] Judges 6:22-23, Judges 13:22, Isaiah 6:5 and other verses
[2] Genesis 18:27
[3] I Kings 19:13
[4] Isaiah 24:23

CHAPTER 2
WHAT IT MEANS TO KNOW GOD

We Must Honor God to Know Him

When I speak of the "knowledge of God," please understand that I mean not only an abstract acknowledgment that God exists, but also a deeper perception of our duty toward Him. We cannot say someone truly *knows* God unless that person demonstrates reverence for God.

Even when we speak of someone truly knowing God, we must be careful of terms. There is one sense in which we *know* God as our Creator, and we understand that He rules over us and provides for us. Yet we may speak of another sense in which we come to *know* Christ as the Redeemer who reconciles lost sinners to God by grace. (Since the Fall, of course, no one could know God in either way unless Christ the Mediator had reconciled God and man). There is a sort of double revelation in Scripture: first, God reveals Himself as Creator, and second, Christ reveals God as our Redeemer. In this first volume, we discuss the role of God as Creator, and in the next, we will examine the role of God as Redeemer.

I have said that we cannot know God unless we reverence Him. But how shall we reverence Him? It is not nearly enough to simply agree that there is a God and that we should honor Him. We must lay hold of the truth that God is the source of every good thing, so that we look for nothing outside of Him. Yes, God keeps the whole universe on course by His power and wisdom. Yes, He rules over all mankind with justice and mercy. But we must know more about Him than that. We must understand that every drop of wisdom, power, goodness, and truth comes from God. We must look to Him for all we need and thank Him for everything we receive. This knowledge of God produces in us a combination of reverence and love which I call "piety." Until we realize that we owe everything to God and that He provides for us like a Father, until we know with certainty that God is the only perfect good in all the universe and everything true and righteous comes from

Him—how can we willingly serve Him? Only when we establish with certainty that real happiness is found solely in God can we truly give ourselves to Him.

Knowledge of God Requires Trust

It is all too common for people to toy with the question, "What is God?" as empty speculation. I have no interest in idle questions. It is far more important for us to study the character and attributes of God than to wonder about His substance. There are some philosophers, such as Epicurus, who would have us believe that God created the world only to lazily toss it aside. How could such a concept of God help us at all?

Our knowledge of God should be characterized by reverent acknowledgement that He created us and that all good things come from Him. If we understand that God created us, then we must recognize that we owe life itself to Him. Since we would not even exist without Him, everything we do should be for Him. Our lives should demonstrate obedience to Him. If we know that He is the source of all good, it should be natural to trust Him and cling to Him.

> **Piety [pahy'-i-tee] - noun**
>
> Calvin uses the word **piety** to describe the combination of reverence and love which compels a believer to willingly obey God.

> **Ancient Philosopher Roll Call**
>
> **Epicurus**
> (341 BC – 270 BC) was an Athenian who founded the ancient school of philosophy known today as Epicureanism. He taught that the ultimate goals in life are self-sufficiency and freedom from fear and pain.
>
> Epicurus told his students that the gods were not involved in the world since they lived far away somewhere. He believed that any religious observance was futile and that human existence ended at death.

A mind truly set on piety (that is, reverence and love for God) should always endeavor to worship God as He has revealed Himself to be. Piety demands that we do not dream up other ideas of God, but rather that we worship the true God and never seek to go beyond what He has commanded. After all, we know that God rules over everything and that He protects us and provides for us. How could we not trust Him?

Since we know that God is the Giver of everything good, we should look to Him for help whenever we are in need. Since we know that He is merciful, we should trust that He will sustain us in trials. Since we know that He is Lord of all, we should obey Him. Since we know that God punishes those who do evil, we should be careful not to provoke Him to anger. However, our fear is not of the sort which would make us run from God (even if we could). We know that God does punish the wicked, but we also know that He is gracious to those who honor and love Him. Furthermore, piety leads us to obey God not merely because we are afraid of punishment, but because He is our Father and our Lord. Even if hell did not exist, those who love God would still tremble at the thought of offending Him.

The pure and real Christian life is this: faith together with fear of God, a fear springing up from willing reverence of God. Such faith carries with it a lawful worship (the worship by which Scripture instructs us to honor God). Nearly everyone has some vague feeling of reverence toward God, but few really serve Him as they should; and wherever there is a lot of showy ceremony in worship, there is very little sincerity of heart.

Them Be Fightin' Words

Calvin takes a jab at Catholicism when he references those who have showy ceremony in worship. The Catholic Church was known for extravagance and excess. Catholic worship often took place in enormous, elaborately-furnished cathedrals and featured luxurious costume, incense, and procession.

Calvin suggests that such extreme focus on the appearance of worship is motivated by a guilty conscience, as a church lacking real sincerity in worship attempts to cover with elaborate showmanship.

CHAPTER 3
OUR INSTINCTIVE KNOWLEDGE OF GOD

Mankind's Natural Tendency to Worship

All people have a natural awareness of the existence of God. This is so obvious that I am not even sure I need to say it. However, I do not want anyone to pretend ignorance on this topic, and so I will say it plainly: God has implanted some awareness of His existence in the minds of all mankind. Therefore, no one has any real excuse for failing to honoring God—everyone knows about Him.

One might imagine that uneducated people or those in remote locations would know nothing at all about God, but it is not so. There is no nation so uncivilized or ignorant that they do not have a strong belief in God. Religion is everywhere—every nation, every city, every household on earth. Even the worship of idols is proof of this innate knowledge of God. We all know how proud and obstinate humans can be. Ordinarily, people tend to turn up their noses at the world and imagine themselves far superior to everyone else. Yet, despite all of that, we see people cast themselves down on their knees in front of wood and stone! People prefer to worship a block of wood rather than worship nothing at all. The conviction of God's existence is deeply and powerfully rooted in the human mind. It can overcome even mankind's obstinate arrogance and compel such strange self-degradation.

Religion is Not a Random Invention

Some philosophers claim that religion is a tool which was invented to keep silly, uneducated people mesmerized. I have even heard it said that people who preach religion to others do not themselves even believe that God exists, but rather they are using it for their own personal gain. I must confess that there have been con artists who like to manipulate others with false reverence or fear of eternal damnation in order to achieve their own purposes. However, if you fully consider

History Corner

Roman Emperor **Gaius Julius Caesar Augustus Germanicus** (12 AD – 41 AD) is commonly called by his childhood nickname **Caligula**. Known for his extreme cruelty, arrogance, and insane behavior, Caligula decreed that all his subjects must worship him as a god. Eventually, Caligula was assassinated by his own guards who conspired with members of the Roman Senate.

Roman historian Suetonius wrote about Caligula: "This man, who so utterly despised the gods, was wont at the slightest thunder and lightning to shut his eyes, to muffle up his head, and if they increased, to leap from his bed and hide under it."

Calvin explains this strange fear as a sign that Caligula knew all too well his own mortality and the terrible judgment that awaited him at the hands of God.

the matter, you must realize that these swindlers would never succeed in this deception unless people were already predisposed to believe in God. Indeed, without the natural inclination to worship, no one would fall for the scam at all.

Some people in the past (and many today) have denied that God exists, but these troubled souls struggle constantly within themselves to overcome their natural propensity to believe. They certainly do not *want* to believe, yet they continually feel a vague premonition which sets them shaking with fear. The Roman Emperor Caligula spewed out contempt against everything religious, and yet no one was more terrified when a hint of God's wrath appeared. Caligula may not have realized the reason for his strange terror, but he was demonstrating his fear of God. Those people who are loudest and most forceful in their rejection of God are the same who tremble even at the rustling of a stray leaf.

The consciences of all mankind testify that God exists and that He sees all. People may run from such knowledge. They may try to wash it out of their thoughts. Yet, in the end, they find themselves trapped by their own minds. Fear rushes in on them again and again. They have no real rest or peace as long as they refuse to acknowledge and serve the Lord.

True Goodness is Impossible

An awareness of God is fixed in the minds of the whole human race. Those who struggle against this fact only further prove it, for they must rage against their natural instincts. Diagoras may make his jokes about religion, and Dionysius may mock the concept of divine judgment, but their laughter is hollow. They are tortured by their own consciences. Mankind may try to banish the knowledge of God, but it always rises again. No one even needs to teach us that God exists. We are born with an innate consciousness of the divine.

Let us consider another angle: if the purpose of every man, woman, and child is to know God, then we are not fulfilling our duty unless every thought and action is fixed firmly upon the knowledge of God. This is not a new idea. The philosopher Plato meant exactly this when he said that the highest good which may be attained by the soul is to grasp the knowledge of God and to be transformed into His likeness. Similarly, Gryllus (in the writings of Plutarch) stated that once people have done away with religion, they are no better than animals. Only in God can we find eternal life, and only in God can we have peace.

Ancient Philosopher Roll Call

The School of Athens
Raffaello Sanzio

Diagoras of Melos was a poet and philosopher in the fifth century BC. He was born in on the island of Melos, but resided in Athens for much of his life. Diagoras is best remembered today for his outspoken atheism. He frequently ridiculed religious observance and attempted to stop others from participating in popular rituals. Ultimately, Diagoras was accused of profaning the Eleusinian mysteries, and he was forced to flee to Corinth, where he died.

Marcus Tullius Cicero (106 BC – 43 BC), a Roman philosopher and statesman, wrote about the tyrant **Dionysius** in Book III of his philosophical dialogue *On the Nature of the Gods*. Cicero reported that Dionysius was commonly in the habit of stealing from the temples and mocking religious devotion. It was rumored that Dionysius would take gold cups and other religious items from the hands of statues of the gods while joking, "It would be folly not to accept good things from the gods, to whom we are constantly praying for favors."

Plato (429 BC – 347 BC) is one of the most influential of all Greek philosophers. He founded the Academy in Athens, and he wrote on a wide range of subjects, including mathematics, art, politics, and religion. Plato challenged traditional Greek religious views by asserting that deity must be perfect in goodness, justice, and beauty.

Plutarch (46 AD – 120 AD) was a Greek historian and writer who became a citizen of the Roman Empire. Plutarch taught a system of ethics closely tied to religion. **Gryllus** was an enchanted pig who appeared as a character in Plutarch's more humorous writings to discuss the ways in which humans are superior to animals.

CHAPTER 4
OUR KNOWLEDGE OF GOD IS DISTORTED

Superstition

God has implanted the knowledge of His existence in the minds of all mankind, and yet this innate awareness is not enough to keep us on the right path. Some people give themselves over to magical thinking and superstition, while others abandon God and deny even His existence.

Superstition is not an innocent theological misunderstanding, however, and we should never excuse it as such. Superstition is what you get when you combine the vague awareness of God's existence with stubborn human pride. People who fall into superstitious deception do so because they never truly seek God. Instead, they twist their concept of God to be more like themselves. They are not worshiping God at all; they are worshiping a figment of their own imaginations. Paul said about such people that "professing to be wise, they became fools," and that they "became futile in their thoughts."[1] Such stupidity of heart and mind cannot be excused, since it is brought about by silly speculation over things which God has not permitted us to know combined with a proud heart which makes people sure that they are always right in their conclusions.

Conscious Turning Away from God

In his psalms, David said that the ungodly and foolish man says in his heart that there is no God.[2] There are people who stupidly set out to extinguish the light which God has given to us. They deliberately confuse themselves and eventually become so hardened in their sin and unbelief that they angrily refuse to think of Him at all. Such people imagine that by denying God's existence, they can avoid judgment. They only wish to carry on untroubled in their wickedness.

---

[1] Romans 1:21-22
[2] Psalm 14:1, 53:1

Some unbelievers may not go as far as completely denying the existence of God, but they still refuse to believe that He is actively involved in the world. Their vague, distant concept of God is nothing like the real God, and so we may still say they are denying God.

A God of Our Imagination

Our human pride makes us yearn to gloss over our errors. We tend to imagine that mere zeal for God is enough. We want to worship God in our own way and to believe that God is happy with our self-centered religion. *True* religion, however, could never be so nonsensically fickle. God is always Himself. He does not change according to whatever each individual person would like Him to be.

The apostle Paul mentions such empty religious fervor when he reminds those in the church that they once worshiped idols. "When you did not know God," he said, "you served those which by nature are not gods." [1] He tells the Ephesians that they were "without God" at the time in which they were wandering from the knowledge of the one true God. [2] Paul does not say they were merely misguided, but rather he declares that they were entirely *without* God. Therefore, I will say (as Lactantius also says) that no religion is genuine unless it is coupled with truth. A religion based upon a false image of God is no true religion at all.

---

[1] Galatians 4:8

[2] Ephesians 2:12

> ### "I'll take 'Obscure Church Fathers' for $900, Alex!"
>
> **Lucius Caelcilius Firmianus Lactantius** (c. 240 AD – c. 320 AD) was a pagan philosopher early in his career. Emperor Diocletian appointed him as professor of rhetoric at Nicomedia. Following his conversion to Christianity, Lactantius was obliged to resign his position. He lived in extreme poverty and had to flee Nicomedia because of persecution .
>
> After the death of Emperor Diocletian, Lactantius regained some of his earlier prominence. Emperor Constantine (the first Christian Roman emperor) hired Lactantius as a tutor for his son Crispus. It is unknown when or how Lactantius died.
>
> Lactantius was an eloquent and gifted writer. He wrote mostly to a pagan audience in an effort to convert them to Christianity. While he succeeded well at proving pagan beliefs wrong, Lactantius was less talented as a Christian theologian. He lacked knowledge or proper understanding of Scripture, and he was sharply criticized by theologians of later generations.
>
> Despite the obvious shortcomings in Lactantius' controversial writings, Calvin expresses appreciation for his argument against false religion. Lactantius boldly proclaimed that paganism was simply unreasonable. A religion based upon lies is no religion at all.

Hypocrisy

Besides the sin of worshiping a god of our own imagination, there is another kind of impiety. Some people prefer not to consider God at all, but when they are forced to acknowledge Him, they do so out of fear of punishment. No real reverence or love for God ever touches their hearts. They live in terror of God's judgment, and yet, if they could have their own way, they would overthrow Him. In order to satisfy both their fear and their rebellious spirit, they make an outward show of religious observance while simultaneously polluting themselves with all manner of evil.

Hypocrisy is a twisting path which appears to approach God while actually running from him. Those who live this way act as if they can satisfy God with a few cheap tokens while indulging themselves in everything that is hateful to Him. This insane behavior can scarcely be called a religion at all, and certainly, it is not anything like the true piety we owe to God.

Over time, hypocrites grow lazier in their pretense of righteousness, and they sin more boldly. Eventually, all sparks of God's light are extinguished within their hearts, and they are completely enslaved by their own wickedness.

From all of this discussion, we can see that mankind has no excuse before God. Everyone knows of God's existence. Everyone knows that God will judge the unrighteous. The only barrier preventing us from true knowledge of God is our own stubborn pride.

CHAPTER 5
THE GLORY OF GOD SHINES AROUND US

God Has Clearly Revealed His Existence to Mankind

Knowing God is the ultimate purpose of all mankind. Everyone has access to this purpose, because (as we have said previously) God has given everyone an inborn awareness of His existence. However, the natural revelation of God's existence does not stop with this instinctive knowledge. God reveals Himself every day in the workings of the universe. When you open your eyes in the morning and see the light of the sun, you are looking on evidence of God's existence. His glory shines out from every corner of creation. As the psalm declares, "O LORD my God, You are very great: You are clothed with honor and majesty, who cover Yourself with light as with a garment." From the first day of creation (the day on which God made light), He showed forth His glory in brilliant splendor. The psalm goes on to say, "He lays the beams of His upper chambers in the waters, who makes the clouds His chariot, who walks on the wings of the wind." [1] Another psalm speaks of the heavens as God's throne.[2] Sparks of God's glory glimmer from every corner of the universe. The whole vast expanse glows with His overwhelming brightness.

David proclaims, "The heavens declare the glory of God; and the firmament shows His handiwork. Day unto day utters speech, and night unto night reveals knowledge. There is no speech nor language where their voice is not heard."[3] The revelation of God is so obvious in His creation that even the most ignorant man or woman should be able to understand. The apostle Paul speaks even more plainly: "What may be known of God is manifest in them, for God has shown it to them. For since the creation of the world His invisible attributes are clearly seen, being understood by the things that are made, even His eternal power and Godhead, so that they are without excuse."[4]

---

[1] Psalm 104:1-3
[2] Psalm 11:4
[3] Psalm 19:1-3
[4] Romans 1:19-20

Without Excuse

In this chapter, Calvin demonstrates that he is well aware of philosophical arguments commonly raised against the exclusivity inherent in the proclamation of one true God and one true faith. He knows that some of his readers will decry this absolute standard as too harsh. It is common for people to grumble that a good God would never punish people for their well-intentioned ignorance.

Calvin combats this complaint by taking a step back and challenging the underlying assumption that ignorance is well-intentioned. After all, everything around us proclaims the glory of God, so why are we still ignorant? Calvin uses an analogy of God setting signs everywhere pointing to the correct path, but we foolish, stubborn creatures still wander away, and then we have the audacity to blame God when we get lost.

Calvin begins and ends this chapter by hammering home the point that mankind has no excuse for failing to know God. God permits no one to remain in a state of blissful ignorance. It is both God's greatest mercy and His greatest judgment on mankind that His glory shines throughout the whole universe. We cannot miss it if we ever for a moment really open our eyes.

Divine Wisdom

It is impossible to count the ways in which God has shown us His great wisdom. I could speak of astronomy, medicine, and other sciences. Every aspect of nature inspires in the scholar a deep admiration for the brilliant design and the Designer. I should not make too much of the sciences, however, for (while it is good to have specialized knowledge about these subjects) one need not even be a scholar in order to witness God's handiwork around us. There is plenty in His magnificent world to fascinate even an uneducated man or woman.

Ancient Philosopher Roll Call

Galen of Pergamon (129 AD – c. 199 AD) was both a physician and a philosopher. Although his understanding of physiology was heavily influenced by the theory of body humors, Galen was able to make some significant advances in the medical field that were remarkable for his era. He also wrote about logic and philosophy, and especially the importance of combining these concepts with the study of medicine.

For example, let us consider the human body. A brilliant physician such as Galen may have had a certain advantage in knowing so much about intricate body systems and how they all work together, but even a simple farmer can look at his own body and marvel at the ingenious design.

How could we claim any honest reason for our failure to know God? We

---

Paul quotes a pagan poet ... did you know it?

The apostle Paul proclaimed the gospel to the Epicurean and Stoic philosophers of Athens. In his speech, he quoted some of their own pagan poets (whose works would have been familiar to his Greek audience) in order to explain some of his points. Calvin mentions one of these poets—Aratus, whom Paul quoted as saying, "We are His offspring" (Acts 17:28). Aratus was a very popular Greek philosopher poet of the third century BC. The line that Paul quoted is taken from *Phaenomena*, a lengthy work concerning stars and weather. The section referenced by Paul reads:

> *Let us begin with Zeus, whom we mortals never leave unspoken.*
> *For every street, every market-place is full of Zeus.*
> *Even the sea and the harbor are full of this deity.*
> *Everywhere everyone is indebted to Zeus.*
> *For we are indeed his offspring.*[1]

By noting Paul's quotation of Aratus, Calvin indirectly reinforces his point in the last chapter that some knowledge of God is instinctive to everyone; even pagan philosophers have some vague awareness of the divine. However, Calvin goes on later to point out that all philosophical exposition about God amounts to little more than foolish rambling. No one can fully know God apart from His revelation in Scripture.

Although unmentioned by Calvin, another pagan poet is also referenced in Acts 17:28. Paul quoted from Epimenides' *Cretica*:

> *But thou art not dead: thou livest and abidest forever,*
> *For in thee we live and move and have our being.*[2]

---

do not even need to look far; our own bodies are marvelous testimonies of God's wisdom and power. Paul said that the knowledge of God is so near to us that we can find it by reaching out to blindly feel for it.[3] If God is so close that we need not even go outside ourselves to find Him, what possible reason could we supply for failing to look even that far?

David praised the glory of God which shines everywhere in creation, and he exclaimed, "What is man that You are mindful of him?" In the same psalm, he said, "Out of the mouths of babes and nursing infants You have ordained strength."[4] David was speaking of the miracle of human existence. A tiny baby cannot even speak a word, and yet the child's whole being proclaims the glory of God. Paul takes this idea one step further when he (quoting Aratus) says that we are God's

---

[1] Aratus, *Phaenomena* 1-5, translated by G.R. Mair.

[2] Epimenides, *Cretica*, translated by J. Rendel Harris.

[3] Acts 17:27

[4] Psalm 8:2, 4

offspring.[1] By bestowing such care in His creation of us, God declares that He is our Father. So evident is this truth from mere observation of ourselves and our world that even secular poets and philosophers refer to God as the Father of mankind.

This is a very important point, because no one can willingly serve God without achieving some comprehension of His fatherly care. Our love for God is a response to His love for us.

Man's Rebellion

Having considered God's kindness and provision, we cannot help but see the terrible ingratitude of mankind. Every person on the face of the earth lives and breathes in a body which was lovingly and brilliantly designed by God. However, instead of bursting out in praise to God, people swell up with pride as though it was their own achievement!

How insane humans can be! They see God's work in their own bodies and souls, and yet they make up some silly excuse about "nature" working out these things. Supposedly, it is "nature" giving men such things as eyes and mouths, language and intelligence. The Epicureans are crazy to spout such nonsense. What random configuration of atoms could gather and cook food, eat and digest it, absorb the useful parts, rid itself of the waste, and gain energy to carry out work? Yet that is only one small part of what the human body can do. Epicurus talks as if all the atoms get together to discuss these things—what alarming stupidity!

I cannot even give serious debate to the bizarre rambling arising from the Epicurean camp. Instead, I will turn to refuting a more subtle error. Aristotle and those who follow him deny immortality, saying that the soul and the body are inextricably bound together so that when the body dies, the soul must die as well.

However, consider for a moment—what concern is it to your body to look up at the sky, to try to count the stars or measure their size and the distance between them? Why would your body care how the planets and stars appear to flow across the sky and whether this one goes a few degrees here or there? I do not mean to emphasize astronomy

> **Remember!**
>
> **Epicureans** were students of **Epicurus**, the Greek philosopher who taught that the gods exist somewhere far away and are not involved in the world; therefore, religious observance would be futile. Calvin used the term to refer to those of his era who generally acknowledged the possibility of God out there somewhere, but believed that humans came into existence through the work of nature. Today we would classify these people as **agnostic**.

---

[1] Acts 17:28

particularly, for there are many possible examples I could have used about man's various contemplations, but in this at least you can see how the soul of man is concerned with many things which have nothing to do with the body. A man may think about heaven or earth, past or future, things he heard long ago, or he may even mentally picture something which he has never seen at all. Even when he is sleeping, his soul rambles around, thinks about things and may even see the future. These are glimpses of an immortal spirit.

How can we gaze at the truth of our own divine origin and yet refuse to acknowledge our Creator? The very gift of knowing right from wrong has been given to us by Him, but we stupidly imagine that God does not know right from wrong and that He will not judge our wicked rejection of Him. Do we think we can defraud the God who gave us all these blessings? We should not be so foolish!

One particular religious group babbles about "secret inspiration" which supposedly gives life to the whole universe. These people love to quote Virgil:

> "First, a spirit within them
> nourishes the sky and earth,
> The watery plains,
> the shining orb of the moon,
> And Titans star, and Mind,
> flowing through matter,
> Vivifies the whole mass
> and mingles with its vast frame.
> From it come the species of man and beast,
> and winged lives,
> And the monsters the sea contains,
> beneath its marbled waves.
> The power of those seeds is fiery,
> and their origin divine."[1]

---

[1] Virgil, Aeneid, Book 6. 724 – 730. Translated by A.S. Kline.

Ancient Philosopher Roll Call

The influence of Greek philosopher **Aristotle** (384 BC – 322 BC) on Western thought has been nearly incalculable, and so it is noteworthy that Calvin makes relatively few references to him in the *Institutes*.

Although obviously influenced by Aristotle's writings on science, Calvin is repulsed by the philosopher's emphatic denial of human immortality.

Aristotle taught that the soul is only found in the activity of the body. From this definition of the soul, Aristotle surmised that when a body becomes irreversibly inactive (dies), the soul ceases to exist.

Calvin argues that the soul gives mankind the capacity to reason; therefore, even the ability to philosophize proves the existence of the soul. If the soul were merely found in movement of the body, then human thought would be entirely consumed with matters related to the function of the body. Furthermore, Calvin asserts that dreams while sleeping prove that the soul is not quenched when the body is inactive.

Of course, this is only a fancy way of saying that the universe somehow created itself! It is doubtful that even Virgil believed this, because elsewhere he said:

> *"Since there is a god in everything,*
> *earth and the expanse of sea and the sky's depths:*
> *from this source the flocks and herds, men, and every species*
> *of creature, each derive their little life, at birth:*
> *to it surely all then return, and dissolved, are remade,*
> *and there is no room for death, but still living*
> *they fly to the ranks of the stars, and climb the high heavens."* [1]

Whatever Virgil believed, let us guard ourselves against such blasphemous babble and all the ungodliness proceeding from it (ungodliness which you can hear in the sacrilegious words of that good-for-nothing Lucretius who always tries to set up some vague pretense of God in place of the real one.)

I will admit that there are some honorable people who may talk about "God in nature" and mean it reverently (for we do see God's work in nature), but I would not recommend using that term at all. There is too much talk these days about nature creating itself or some such nonsense, and people may be confused even by the use of such a phrase.

God's Sovereignty

In all this discussion, I aim to establish firmly that whenever we think of ourselves, we must acknowledge our Creator. We must always remember that there is one God who governs the whole universe. He has commanded that we direct our faith toward Him, worshiping only Him and praying only to Him. After all, nothing would be sillier than to enjoy all the wonderful gifts which He bestows on us every day while ignoring the One who generously gives them.

---

[1] Virgil, *Georgics*, Book IV. 219-227.
Translated by A.S. Kline.

"I Just Can't Stand It!"

Despite Calvin's earlier comment that he would not even bother to respond to Epicurean babbling, he appears to have found the quarrel irresistible. "Those who love to quote Virgil" were indeed the Epicureans, for whom **Lucretius** (c. 99 BC – c. 55 BC) was the chief philosophical expositor and **Virgil** (70 BC – 19 BC) the admired poet.

Epicureanism, which had mostly died out in the Middle Ages, revived again during the Renaissance with the rediscovery of Lucretius' philosophical poem *On the Nature of Things*.

Various offshoots of the philosophy developed, including contemporaries of Calvin (such as Erasmus) who attempted to reconcile Epicurean philosophy with Christianity.

We must know that it is God who sustains heaven and earth by His Word. God sends the thunder that shakes the earth and the lightning that scorches the ground, and God clears it away again in a moment. God orders the wind that sweeps the sea into a roaring fury, and then He calms the storm. Everything is created and governed by Him.

However, it is not merely in such mighty works of nature that we see God's power. God's sovereign goodness orders human society so that we naturally tend to reward the righteous and punish the wicked. People are inclined to brood over the temporary triumph of the wicked or the suffering of the righteous, and yet these are exceptions to an overall general principle of justice in society. (Criminals are usually punished, not rewarded.) Perhaps "exceptions" is a poor word for it, since we know that those sinners who seem to get away with their wickedness in this life will not really go unpunished forever; there will be another judgment beyond the earthly courts. In the end, there will be no exceptions.

As we think on God's justice, let us not neglect to think on His mercy as well. We marvel not only that He punishes evil, but also that He often pursues miserable sinners with inexhaustible kindness until He shatters their obstinate wickedness with His fatherly love and brings them back to Himself.

The psalmist tells us of many occasions when people who seemed to be beyond all hope cried out to God and found help: God protected those wandering in the desert and guided them back home, God supplied the hungry with food, God freed prisoners from dungeons, God protected the shipwrecked, God cured those afflicted with disease, and many more. God raises up the humble, and He casts down the proud.[1] By showing us so many examples, the psalmist explains that events which appear to be merely good luck are actually proof of God's providence, and especially of His fatherly love.

So let us be encouraged, for we know that God gives joy to the righteous and breaks the strength of the proud and wicked. God does everything well and always at the right time. He "makes foolish the wisdom of this world" when "He catches the wise in their own craftiness."[2] In the end, God works everything for good.

Our Contemplation of God

It is clear that there is no great difficulty in setting out proofs of God's existence and majesty. We have looked at a few already, but, truthfully, the

---

[1] Psalm 107:4-7, 9, 10-16, 23-30, 17-20, 39-41

[2] I Corinthians 1:20, 3:19

evidence is all around us, and I am certain that the reader can think of many more examples. However, I would like to point out again that a mere acknowledgement of God's existence is insufficient to say we know God. The knowledge of God must take root in our hearts and bear fruit, or else it is no use at all.

If God had never bothered to show us His glory, then we might be excused for having little enthusiasm for seeking Him. But since we see His revelation shining everywhere, we must be profoundly affected by it. We must seek to know more about Him. However, we should do so in reverence, seeking Him only in the way in which He has permitted us to find Him. It is inappropriate for humans to speculate about God's essence. Instead, we should contemplate His works, because they are a sort of communication to us. Paul referred to this when he said that we need not look for God far away, for "in Him we live and move and have our being."[1] David spoke of God's works and then said that he would declare God's greatness.[2] Considering these Scriptures, we know that this sort of meditation is a very proper way to seek God. After all, we cannot begin to fathom the true greatness of God. Any attempt to understand Him in all His fullness would merely discourage us. Instead, we should gaze on His works, so that we may be strengthened by His goodness.

Knowledge of God causes us to worship God, of course, but it also encourages us in the hope of life after death. We see in this world a very incomplete picture of God's mercy and justice, and so we know

> **History Corner**
>
> **Augustine of Hippo** (354 AD – 430 AD) was born in a Roman African province. His father Patricius was a pagan, but his mother Monica was a devout Christian. Monica prayed for her son's conversion for many years, and her prayers were answered in 386 AD. Augustine wrote later that he was at that time in a deep spiritual crisis, and he heard a childlike voice telling him, "Take up and read." He picked up Paul's epistle to the Romans and began to read it. The transformation in Augustine's life was instantaneous and profound. He devoted the rest of his life to studying and teaching theology. He wrote some of the most influential works in the history of the church.
>
> Calvin and the other Reformers greatly admired Augustine. Both Luther and Calvin quoted Augustine more than they quoted any other theologian. So pervasive was the influence of Augustine on the Reformed understanding of the doctrine of grace that B.B. Warfield later declared, "It is Augustine who gave us the Reformation."[3]

---

[1] Acts 17:28

[2] Psalm 145:3-6

[3] Warfield, *Calvin and Augustine*, Pennsylvania: The Presbyterian and Reformed Publishing Company, 1956.

there are greater things still to come. We know that God is righteous, and so when we look around us and see injustice, we must conclude that death is not the end of everything. Remember Augustine's words: "If God punished every sin immediately, then nothing would be reserved for the last judgment. On the other hand, if God never punished sin in this life, then everyone would think that He does not care for us at all."[1]

We may think of God's work of creation like a painting. God places before us a picture of His power and glory, and He invites all mankind to look and find their happiness in Him. However, in order for us to understand why we are given this picture and to appreciate the true value of it, we must turn our thoughts more inward to ponder the ways in which God has demonstrated His life, mercy, and power in us and for us.

The Futility of Philosophy Without God

God shows us a sort of picture or reflection of Himself in His works, but humans are dense creatures who fail to see what He has put before our eyes. We become so accustomed to seeing His wonders that we rarely pause to consider them or ponder what they mean for us. In fact, we tend to think of ourselves as tossed around by blind fortune rather than governed by God's providence. All of us occasionally have a few thoughts about God, but we are quick to fall back into error almost immediately because of our sin and pride. We humans may have many differences between us, but we are all very much alike in that we forsake the true God for things which really do not matter at all. This characteristic is like a disease infecting every man, woman, and child on earth, no matter whether they are intelligent or stupid, well-educated or unschooled.

> ### Plato Runs in Circles
>
> In his dialogue *Timaeus*, Plato states that God is the Maker of the world, but then he departs into bizarre speculation. He suggests that God made the earth spherical (a "round globe," Calvin says) so that it would be perfect like Himself, and that God also gave it a soul. In short, *Timaeus* argues that the world itself is a living being.

The whole tribe of philosophers has produced nothing but proof that this is true. Their foolishness is embarrassing! Some silly writings may be dismissed as mere ramblings of ignorant men, but how do we account for Plato? He was otherwise a brilliant and deeply religious man, and yet he got lost in his own "round globe." If this is how our philosophers and teachers act, imagine the effect on the rest of us! These men were supposed to be our shining lights leading the way!

---

[1] Augustine, *City of God*, Book I, Chapter 8.

With the whole world mired in error, each person's mind is a maze of confusion. No wonder then that whole cities and nations—and indeed every individual soul—has its own gods. Scarcely has there ever been a person who did not make an idol or fantasy god for himself in the place of the real God. Just as water bubbles up from a spring, so does an immense crowd of gods flow from the human mind. Each person (filled with self-importance) wrongly invents all sorts of things about God which have no basis in reality. I cannot even begin to describe all the mistakes people have made about God; there would be no end to this chapter if I tried to do that.

I want to be very clear that intelligence gets people no nearer to God. You might think that philosophers who have tried to reason their way to heaven might at least have attained a better grasp of the nature of God than less educated people. But if you really read their eloquent writings, you find only confusion and error under all the lovely words. The Stoics imagined themselves to be completely brilliant in their claim that gods drawn from all parts of nature were somehow unified into one—as if we do not already have enough problems without being encouraged to invent more gods! The mystical religion of the Egyptians, which was

> **Ancient Philosopher Roll Call**
>
> Greek philosopher **Zeno** founded the philosophy that became known as **Stoicism**.
>
> Stoics believed that a divine presence could be found everywhere and that the universe was somehow unified into one vast living thing.
>
> According to this philosophy, souls would be absorbed into the great universal consciousness at death.

contemplated for thousands of years, was every bit as corrupt as any new philosophy. No one has ever gotten far in their comprehension of God merely by thinking, no matter how long or how carefully they have thought.

All of this crazy variation in religion does nothing but embolden the Epicureans and others who despise religion. They use it as an excuse to throw out God altogether. They read all the philosophers who theorize this and that, all disagreeing with each other. Finally, the Epicureans conclude that people only torment themselves looking for a god who cannot be found and may not even exist. They would rather have the sense of certainty achieved by proclaiming there is no god than to be unsure whether this person or that person is right about God.

People disagree more about religion than about any other topic in the world. The blindness of humanity is painfully obvious as we all meander hopelessly around — guessing this and hypothesizing that — and yet more stupid and blind than ever. Some say that Simonides answered best about God when he was asked by the tyrant Hiero concerning the nature of God, and he begged to be given a day to

---

The More I Think, the Less I Understand ...

By comparing the various views on God held by philosophers, Calvin points out that there is nothing remotely resembling a consensus. Philosophers—who might be brought to some basic agreement about subjects such as math or science—cannot even form a coherent concept of God. Some claim that there are many gods (each with a unique personality), while others postulate that everything in the universe is unified into a single divine spirit.

In his work *The Nature of the Gods*, Roman philosopher **Cicero** tells the tale of **Simonides** and **Hiero** which Calvin references in this chapter. Cicero relates the story in order to acknowledge his own uncertainty about the nature of the divine. He concludes, "Simonides, who was not only a delightful poet, but reputed a wise and learned man in other branches of knowledge, found, I suppose, so many acute and refined arguments occurring to him, that he was doubtful which was the truest, and therefore despaired of discovering any truth."[1]

Calvin agrees with Cicero that Simonides' answer is the only honest response for someone who does not know God through Scripture. With only the light of nature, even the most intelligent person may know nothing certain about God and can only grasp the vaguest idea of His existence. Humans are constantly led astray by their own compulsion to fashion a god according to their own wishes. Without the Word of God, we all must (as Cicero said) despair of discovering any truth.

---

consider his answer. When the next day arrived, he asked for two days more, and then for still more time. Finally, he could only say, "The more I think about this, the less I understand it." And perhaps, after all, that is the most accurate answer he could have given. When people look only at nature for their revelation of God, they cannot hold on to anything certain. Ultimately, the altar in their hearts bears the inscription, "TO THE UNKNOWN GOD."[2]

No Excuse

All who corrupt pure religion (and this is inevitable when each person follows his or her own opinion) separate themselves from the one true God. People might say they have no bad intentions about it, but that does not matter. The Holy Spirit rejects all who worship demons in the place of God. Scripture makes very plain that there is only one God whom we should honor and that all other gods are false. The only divine presence was on Mount Zion where the true knowledge of God flourished. God did not acknowledge any pagan sacrifice as legitimate worship. During Christ's life on earth, the Samaritans seemed to be the closest to true reverence of God, and yet Jesus said the Samaritans did not know what they

---

[1] Cicero, *The Nature of the Gods*, XXII. Translated by C. D. Yonge.

[2] Acts 17:23

worshiped, suggesting that they were suffering serious delusion.[1]

There is no such thing as a "good religion" which is based entirely on human reason. It is certainly no surprise that the Holy Spirit rejects all religions invented by humans; all humans judge by their own opinions and never reach anything resembling the truth about God.

Some people (especially civil administrators and legislators) promote the idea that everyone should worship whichever deity has been traditionally honored by his ancestors. Indeed, Socrates praised the oracle of Apollo for declaring that everyone should follow the religion of his or her own city. What sort of custom is that? Are we going to simply rely on the judgment of other people on such a serious matter? Will we toss evidence and reason aside and run after whatever someone else says we should do? This argument is far too weak. We cannot rely on our ancestors and hope they happened to guess correctly about God. We must look to God Himself for our answers.

Nature is full of the revelation of God, and yet it is poured out on us in vain. We are standing in a floodlight of God's glory, but we

---

History Corner

The **Oracle of Apollo** was located at Delphi in ancient Greece, and it was so famous that people from all around the Mediterranean traveled to inquire there about all manner of decisions. Questions were brought to a priestess called Pythia who sat over a fissure in the earth, inhaling gases which bubbled up through the crack. She would fall into a drugged trance and mutter incoherently. Priests of Apollo would "translate" the messages for inquirers—messages which were often vague and could be interpreted in various ways.

Greek philosopher **Socrates** (c. 469 BC – 399 BC) reportedly admired the words of the Oracle in regard to proper worship of the gods. Xenophon, a student of Socrates, recorded in his book *Memorabilia* that whenever someone would go to the temple to make an inquiry about proper religious observance, "the priestess replies that *they will act piously, if they act in agreement with the law of their country*; and Socrates both acted in this manner himself, and exhorted others to act similarly."[2]

Socrates apparently took the Oracle's statement to mean that the gods honor all lawful sacrifice. More likely, it was an attempt by the priests at Delphi to ensure that the Temple did not run afoul of civil authorities.

The ruins of the temple of Apollo at Delphi

---

[1] John 4:22

[2] Xenophon, *Memorabilia*, Book I, Chapter III.

cannot follow it to the right path. Sometimes a stream of light briefly penetrates the darkness of our souls, but pride snuffs it out almost instantly.

Paul teaches that those things which may be known of God have been made plain since the creation of the world, and yet he only says this in order to prove that mankind is without any excuse for ignorance.[1] Paul also says that God is near to everyone, but he then adds: "...the living God, who made the heaven, the earth, the sea, and all things that are in them, who in bygone generations allowed all nations to walk in their own ways. Nevertheless He did not leave Himself without witness, in that He did good, gave us rain from heaven and fruitful seasons, filling our hearts with food and gladness."[2] This Bible passage tells us that God has left a witness of Himself for everyone through His works of providence, and it also observes that the testimony of nature is ineffective at turning the hearts of mankind. Despite the blessings poured from God's hand, all nations continue to walk in their own way.

Although we cannot rise up to know God through the testimony of His creation, we cannot excuse ourselves either. Our own spiritual blindness and stupidity prevents us from attaining that knowledge. We cannot claim that we are innocently mistaken when every sign points to the right way and yet we still manage to wander away. However our error arises—whether we twist our understanding of God according to our own imagination or whether we pretend to honor Him while carrying out great evil or whether we act as though we can judge His works and complain of His providence—all of these turn our hearts away from worship of the true God. We are without excuse.

---

[1] Romans 1:19
[2] Acts 14:15-17

CHAPTER 6
SCRIPTURE TEACHES US TO KNOW GOD

Scripture Guides Us to God

The knowledge of God's existence is instinctive to all of us, and His glory shines around us so that we are without any excuse for ignorance. However, these natural revelations are never enough to overcome sinful human pride. Something more must be given to us, and so God gave us His Word.

God saw that the minds of all mankind were confused and lost, and so He chose a people for Himself—the people of Israel. He fenced them in so that they would not wander away. The pure light of the Word grasped their hearts and held them up so that they could not fall completely, and He holds us the same way. Without Scripture, we would never be able to stand firm in the true knowledge of God.

Let me suggest an illustration. Suppose there is an old man whose eyes have grown very weak. Perhaps a friend brings him a book and says, "You should read this, sir! It is a wonderful book!" No matter how hard he tries, the elderly man cannot see the words. There is a defect within him which literally blinds him to the knowledge contained in the book, even though it is right in front of him. Then, suppose the friend gives the old man his reading glasses. With the help of those glasses, the words which were so impossible see a moment ago now come into sharp focus. He can read the whole book. The reading glasses are like the Bible. Without the Word of God, we cannot understand anything about God, even though evidence of God's existence and character is right before our eyes. With the help of Scripture, we see clearly, and we are able to know God.

Remember that I previously noted that there are two types of knowledge. I want to clarify the distinction between them. I am not yet speaking of the faith which illuminates the heart when we know Christ as our Redeemer. Before we can reach that point, we must recognize God as the One who created the universe and rules over everything. When we know God as Creator, then we come to know Him

---

Eyeglasses for the World

In the first five chapters of the *Institutes*, Calvin emphasizes the glory of God revealed in nature. In the sixth chapter, however, his argument begins to turn. He has proven that we all are without excuse for our failure to know God. Yet, as fallen creatures, none of us could possibly know God unless He had reached down to help us.

We are defective, Calvin declares. His analogy is one of an old man with poor eyesight who cannot read a book set in front of him. The knowledge is right there before our eyes, but we cannot make sense of it.

In the next few chapters, Calvin proclaims the centrality of the Scripture to the Christian faith. The Word and the Spirit together are the help from heaven which we so desperately need. The Word is our pair of eyeglasses through which we can finally make sense of the world around us and know its Creator. The Spirit illumines us to understand and obey the Scriptures.

Calvin accepts no revelation besides the Word of God. He is a staunch cessationist, declaring that prophecies and visions have ended now that the Scriptures are complete.

---

also as our Redeemer. In time, I will discuss the covenant which God made with Abraham and his descendants. However, in this section, my primary aim is to establish with certainty that God is our Creator, and that He is not like any of the multitude of false gods. With that qualification in mind, let us proceed to a discussion of the revelation of God in Scripture.

The Word of God

It is not entirely clear to us how all the patriarchs arrived at their knowledge of God, and, in fact, the method was not even the same for all of them. For some, prophecies and visions seem to have led the way, while, for others, instruction provided the key to understanding the truth of God. However it happened, it is obvious that these men were certain that the things which they had learned came ultimately from God Himself. The Word of God removes the plague of uncertainty, and it establishes faith beyond speculation.

God ordained that the message conveyed to the patriarchs should be written down in order to ensure that it would remain unchanged through generations. God's law was never a secret; God directed that it should be openly proclaimed so that all His people would hear and obey. After the law was given, He sent the prophets to interpret and apply it.

Scripture sets forth both types of knowledge of God—that He is our Creator and our Redeemer. Even though I said earlier that we should contemplate the works of God to know Him better (and we should), the best way to know Him is through His Word. No one can gain even the slightest sense of proper doctrine without studying Scripture.

We begin to know God when we reverently accept the generous gift of knowledge found in His Word. We know God when we obey Him, and we first obey Him by welcoming Scripture as the means by which we may know Him.

Without Scripture, We Will Certainly Fall Away

The human mind is always a fragile thing. How easily we forget and fall away from truth! How quickly we create fantasy gods to worship! We can see why God chose to have His Word written down for us. Otherwise, how could the true knowledge of God ever survive through centuries? The written Word stands before us always the same, always free of the forgetful and ever-shifting influence of human thought.

In order to truly know God, we must approach Him in His Word so that we avoid the temptation to evaluate Him by our own corrupt opinions. Scripture forces us to view Him in the light of His everlasting truth. Our minds change, but He never changes. Through Scripture, we are brought back again and again to see Him as He really is. If we wander off the path which He has set out for us, then no matter how fast we go or how hard we try, we will never end up where we intended. Without the guidance of God's Word, any study of the divine is like a maze in which we instantly become hopelessly lost. It is far better to barely hobble along the true path than to race along in the wrong direction.

David often teaches in his psalms that God reigns. David speaks not so much of God's power over nature as of Him reigning as King in our hearts. Error can never be forced out of the human heart unless truth replaces and rules over it.

Scripture Reveals God to Us

We mentioned in the previous section that David proclaims God's authority. David also praises God's glory as revealed in nature: "The heavens declare the glory of God; and the firmament shows His handiwork. Day unto day utters speech, and night unto night reveals knowledge."[1] Having just said that, however, David

---

[1] Psalm 19:1-2

continues in the same psalm, "The law of the LORD is perfect, converting the soul; the testimony of the LORD is sure, making wise the simple; the statutes of the LORD are right, rejoicing the heart; the commandment of the LORD is pure, enlightening the eyes." [1] Although the heavens declare the glory of God, the eyes of His children are enlightened by Scripture.

We may easily find other examples of this principle in the Bible. Psalm 29 tells us that God's voice thunders over the waters and in the forests, and yet in the end, it concludes: "In His temple everyone says, "Glory!"[2] God is worshipped in His Temple where the Word is taught. Similarly, Psalm 93 speaks of the waves of the sea lifting up their voice, and yet the last verse of the psalm reads: "Your testimonies are very sure; holiness adorns Your house, O LORD, forever."[3] Again, God's revelation in nature is mighty, but the house of God is where the testimony of God is sure. Finally, let us consider the words of Christ when He spoke to the Samaritan woman: "You worship what you do not know; we know what we worship, for salvation is of the Jews."[4]

Unless the human mind is guided by Scripture, it can never rise to a place of knowing God. Only through God's Word can we fully know Him. All who seek God in other paths are doomed to stumble blindly.

---

[1] Psalm 19:7-8

[2] Psalm 29:9

[3] Psalm 93:5

[4] John 4:22

CHAPTER 7
THE AUTHORITY OF SCRIPTURE

The Authority of Scripture is from God

Before I go on to other matters, I want to devote a few pages to a discussion of the authority of Scripture. It is very important for my readers to believe that the Bible is the Word of God. We cannot make any headway unless that principle is set as absolute. There is no point in discussing theology with anyone who does not acknowledge the authority of God's Word.

No prophecy descends to us today straight from heaven, for it has pleased the Lord to give us His eternal truth in Scripture alone. We should always bear in mind that God speaks to us today in His Word. Only when we remember this rule will we reverence the Scriptures as we should.

The topic of the authority of Scripture deserves more than the passing attention that I shall give it, but (due to the great variety of topics we must cover in this book) I cannot look into it as thoroughly as I would like. At present, we will touch only upon the basics.

In doing so, we must minimally consider the serious error which has become so popular lately—the idea that Scripture has only as much importance as the church agrees to give it. I can scarcely even imagine why this error has become so common! Do we really suppose that the truth of God depends upon our own judgment of it? Do we really think we can take a little of this and a little of that as we please and throw the rest away?

Those who cast doubt on Scripture mock the Holy Spirit with such impertinent questions! They ask, "Who can know for sure whether these words came from God? How do we know whether it has changed over time? Wouldn't it be better for the church to make decisions about which parts of the Bible are important for us today?"

What dreadful deception we plunge into when we spew such nonsense! How could anyone have assurance of salvation or feel any sense of stability if the

---

"I Just Listen to the Pope!"

During the Reformation, many Roman Catholics clung tightly to the decrees of the pope and refused to consider arguments from Scripture. Some dismissed Scripture as unreliable and riddled with error. They declared that they were unable to decipher the meaning of it themselves or even to know which parts were correct. For these decisions, they relied on the Catholic Church.

Calvin decries this notion as absurd, pointing out that the church has its authority from Scripture, and so Scripture must be superior to the opinion of whoever happens to be in leadership of the church at the moment.

Calvin's frustration at the absurdity of such a view is mingled with pity. He ponders how such people can possibly find stability and assurance of salvation. After all, popes have frequently contradicted each other. Things accepted by the Catholic Church one minute might be outlawed the next. How could anyone feel certain of their salvation under those circumstances? To them, the laws of God must always appear as shifting shadows, carried along by human whims.

Scripture is not so desperately unstable. It stands unchanged and secure forever, and its authority is directly from God Himself. In the end, the pope does not judge the Word; the Word judges the pope.

Bible could not even be trusted? We cannot promote a system which makes humans the ultimate authority. God is trustworthy; humans are not.

The Church Receives Its Authority from Scripture

It is a simple and straightforward matter to refute the claim that the authority of the church is superior to the authority of Scripture. The apostle Paul states that the church is "built on the foundation of the apostles and prophets."[1] If the apostles and prophets are the foundation, then their authority was already established before the church even existed. Without Scripture, there would be no church at all.

Of course, the church does proclaim the truth of Scripture, but not as though it was in doubt until the church approved it. The church recognizes the truth of the Word of God, and that is why we proclaim it. There are some who might say, "How can we know that the Bible is true until the church says so?" But this question is nonsense! How do you know whether light is different from darkness without the commentary of the church? How can you differentiate sweet from bitter without church approval? The Word of God proves itself.

---

[1] Ephesians 2:20

Dueling the Dualists

Manichaeism thrived between the third and seventh centuries AD. Founded by an Iranian named Mani, the belief system incorporated ideas from several religions, including Christianity. Manichees claimed that Christianity (and other religions) had corrupted and misunderstood spiritual truth and that the Manichees alone retained complete understanding. They were fond of dismissing their opponents by merely stating that Manichees had knowledge of the Scriptures which no one else possessed.

Manichaeism taught a gnostic and dualistic view of the universe. They viewed matter as evil and spirit as good, and they believed the universe was caught in a battle between those good and evil forces.

Augustine of Hippo was originally a Manichee before converting to Christianity. Following his conversion, he condemned Manichaeism for flattering its adherents with a feeling of righteousness while failing to truly change the hearts of sinners. He also emphasized the authority of the church in order to shame those Manichees who believed themselves to possess secret knowledge unavailable to larger Christendom.

Catholics and Protestants alike deeply respected Augustine and wanted to claim him as their own. Catholics often pointed to Augustine's appeal for the Manichees to respect the church as evidence that the church's authority was absolute, even over Scripture. Calvin dismissed this interpretation of Augustine and indicated that the Catholics were taking Augustine's words out of context.

The Augustine Controversy

Augustine made a statement which is often quoted by those who are looking to place the authority of the church over the authority of Scripture. He said that he would not believe even the gospel unless it was supported by the testimony of the church.[1]

Augustine has been treated most unfairly, however, by those who involve him in this debate. His comment has been taken wildly out of context. Augustine was talking about the Manichees, who were fond of making big claims which they could not prove. The Manichees would say that the Bible supported their view as if that settled everything with no further questions. Augustine wondered, "What would the Manichees do if they met someone who did not believe the Bible? How could they possibly try to convince anyone if the only persuasive tool they possess is saying, 'The Bible is on my side'?" Then he continued by saying that he would not accept the gospel without the testimony of the church. In other words, Augustine

---

[1] Augustine, *Against the Epistle of Manichaeus Called Fundamental*, Chapter IV.

meant that, if he were an unbeliever, he would not be persuaded of the truth of the gospel without the testimony of the church. He was not attempting to comment about the authority of the church in comparison to the Bible at all! He only intended to say that those who are without Christ are led to consider Scripture in a new and compelling way by the witness of the church.

This point is much clearer in Augustine's subsequent statements to the Manichees: "You cannot prove either of your points. You merely praise your beliefs and ridicule mine. So, after I have taken my own turn at praising my beliefs and ridiculed yours, where are we? Ultimately, we should part company with people who promise they will reveal great knowledge beyond all doubt and then demand faith in very doubtful things. We should follow instead those who invite us to begin by believing in something which we cannot fully understand, so that, when we are strengthened in this faith, we may come to a place where we believe by the inward illumination and confirmation of our minds—a persuasion no longer by the proofs of man but by God Himself."[1]

These are Augustine's own words, and it is easy to see what he really meant: the testimony of the church is an introduction to the gospel for unbelievers. Certainly, Augustine had great respect for the church. Augustine would plead with people who thought they had their own personal revelation from God. He would remind them that the church had considered these things for centuries and so we should not blithely toss aside the wisdom of generations of godly souls for some uncertain new idea. However, it would never have occurred to Augustine to suggest that the authority of the Word of God rests on the whim of the church.

If my readers would like more proof of this, I would urge them to read Augustine's booklet *The Usefulness of Belief*. In this work, Augustine makes it very clear that the church helps us interpret Scripture and gives us direction in study, but Augustine adds that we should settle our beliefs only on the sure Word of God, not on the opinions of others.

The Testimony of the Holy Spirit

Ultimately, we will never be persuaded of the authority of Scripture until we are sure that God Himself is the Author. When you read the Bible, you will notice that the prophets and apostles did not boast about their credentials or intelligence.

---

[1] Augustine, *Against the Epistle of Manichaeus Called Fundamental*, Chapter XIV.

They did not spend a lot of time trying to prove anything. They simply spoke the Word of God.

Certainly, there are rational human proofs by which we can be certain that the Law, the Prophets, and the Gospels all must come from God, but none of these compare to the quiet testimony of the Holy Spirit in our hearts.

Some very intelligent and well-educated men have risen up with the intention of disproving Scripture, only to ultimately admit they see signs that God is speaking through Scripture. How could this be unless the Scriptures were from heaven? If those who are so determined to disprove God could be brought to such an admission, then surely anyone who approaches the Bible with reverence and humility will immediately see God's majesty and obey Him.

Some Christians think they can convert many souls by arguing with unbelievers. I have never found it to be much use. Certainly, it is possible to prove the authority of Scripture, but then what have you accomplished? There is no way to change the hearts of people who are determined not to believe. They merely reply, "But I think ..." and that is the end of it. Their opinions outweigh even the clearest evidence placed before them. Unless the Holy Spirit changes the heart, the mind will not change.

> **A man convinced against his will**
> **Is of the same opinion still.**
>
> This old proverb warns us that beliefs are often based on emotion rather than good evidence. People tend to believe whatever they want to believe, regardless of any evidence against it.
>
> Calvin also warns of this stubborn streak in human nature: "There is no way to change the heart of someone who is determined not to believe."

The prophet Isaiah spoke of the testimony of the Spirit in our hearts: "'As for Me,' says the LORD, 'this is My covenant with them: My Spirit who is upon you, and My words which I have put in your mouth, shall not depart from your mouth, nor from the mouth of your descendants, nor from the mouth of your descendants' descendants,' says the LORD, 'from this time and forevermore.'"[1]

A few well-meaning Christians are inclined to be annoyed with anyone who is not prepared at a moment's notice to argue about the authority of the Bible with any unbeliever who says something against it. It would be good for them to remember that the Holy Spirit is the seal and guarantee of our faith.[2] Until the Spirit illuminates the mind, a doubter will never cease to doubt.

---

[1] Isaiah 59:21

[2] II Corinthians 1:22

Scripture Proves Itself

Let me make this point very clear: Scripture does not need external proof. Those whom God has called will rest upon His Word by the illumination of the Spirit. Scripture proves itself, and it is wrong to analyze it as though it were any ordinary work of literature or philosophy. Even without the prompting of the Holy Spirit, the majesty of Scripture may be acknowledged, but so what? We can only obey the Word of God by the work of the Spirit upon our hearts. Until God prompts us to hear Him, we cannot ever be talked into faith.

Those whom the Spirit has prompted will never need to prove Scripture in any other way. Their perspective has changed so that they judge their own thoughts and opinions by Scripture, rather than judge Scripture by their own thoughts and opinions. This does not mean that believers are blind in their faith. In perfect clarity of thought, Christians seize upon the eternal truth of God in a manner which is far beyond human opinion. We obey God willingly and knowingly, but in a way that is above human knowing and willing.

In Book III, I will discuss more fully the testimony and work of the Holy Spirit, and so I will put this topic aside for now. In the meantime, let me say that true faith is that which is sealed in our hearts by the Holy Spirit. The elect believe, and yet a vast multitude of others will never believe, no matter how much proof is set before them. Isaiah warned that his prophetic word would not be understood or believed by everyone, asking, "To whom has the arm of the LORD been revealed?"[1] Whenever we are discouraged by how few believe the gospel, let us remember that only those whom God has chosen will ever understand the mysteries of God.

---

[1] Isaiah 53:1

CHAPTER 8
SCRIPTURE ABOVE HUMAN WISDOM

Scripture is Superior to Human Wisdom

We can admire many things about the Bible—the wisdom of its organization, the wonderful agreement of its parts with one another, the heavenly nature of its doctrine. Our hearts are more amazed when we realize that something more than eloquence of speech draws us to read Scripture. In fact, much of the Bible is written in very plain speech, and God ordained that it should be so. No one can claim that believers are captured by fancy language. It is the will of God that the spectacular truth of the divine is conveyed to us in utmost simplicity, so we may know that the power of Scripture is the force of truth. The apostle Paul commented on this when he said to the Corinthians, "My speech and my preaching were not with persuasive words of human wisdom, but in demonstration of the Spirit and of power, that your faith should not be in the wisdom of men but in the power of God."[1] Truth is cleared of all doubt when it is so powerful that it serves as its own proof and does not need anything else to support it.

There have been many eloquent human writers. If you wish to see graceful writing, then read Demosthenes, Cicero, Plato, or Aristotle. These were all talented men whose words will thrill you. But then set those books aside and pick up the Bible. You will discover that Scripture pierces you to the heart in a manner which the words of philosophers never can. Scripture, even in its often simple language, breathes something divine.

Variety of Style

I will admit that some of the prophets were very elegant in their writing. It is not as though I am saying that the pagan philosophers surpass all of the prophets in

---

[1] I Corinthians 2:4-5

writing style. The Holy Spirit demonstrated that He could be eloquent, even as He proved He could be simple and direct. David and Isaiah were gifted with words. Amos, Jeremiah, and Zechariah had a more rustic tone. Through it all, the glory of God shines eternally.

We should not make a false distinction, as though anything lovely is pagan and anything simple is divine. Satan is an imitator of God's work, and people have been deceived in both directions—drawn in by lovely words or by the most unsophisticated teaching. Let us not be such fools as to think everything unrefined is inspired by God.

In regard to the Bible, however, let us conclude that no matter how the enemies of God try to chip away at it, it stands unmoved. It is filled from cover to cover with thoughts which could not possibly be human in origin. Look at any of the prophets for an example; all of them far exceed anything humans could achieve. If someone finds the prophets tasteless, then all I can say is that such a person must lack taste buds.

The Prophets: Princes and Paupers

The Old Testament prophets were an unlikely assortment of characters. Moses had been a prince in Egypt, Zechariah was a priest, and Amos was a simple shepherd. Some were exiles in Babylon, while others were held captive in their own country.

The writing styles of the books of the Bible are as varied as the human authors who penned them. Isaiah's eloquence is so pronounced that he is sometimes referred to as the "Shakespeare of the prophets."[1] Amos employs simple, forceful language to convey God's message.

Calvin points to these stylistic differences as proof of the authority of Scripture. Despite such a wide range of styles, the message remains the same. The impact of the Word is not in sweet language or in rough tone, but rather in the truth contained within it. Scripture rises above ordinary tools of human persuasion.

---

[1] Willmington, Harold, "Isaiah: Shakespeare of the Prophets" (1985). *Articles.* Paper 13.

CHAPTER 9
WORD AND SPIRIT

The Insanity of Heresy

Some people who endeavor to find God outside of Scripture could be considered crazy rather than deceived. These days, there are unbalanced people who brazenly teach blatant heresy. They claim to be filled with the Spirit, and they despise anyone who studies Scripture and theology. They dismiss everyone who reads the Bible as "following the dead letter."

Since they declare themselves led by the "spirit," I would really like to ask them what sort of spirit would dare to look down on the Word of God. If they answer that it is the Spirit of Christ leading this revolution against the Bible, then they are simply ridiculous. They would agree that Jesus and the apostles were filled with the Holy Spirit. How can they fail to notice that Jesus and the apostles all held Scripture in the very highest esteem?

The prophet Isaiah spoke of the Word and the Spirit: "'As for Me,' says the LORD, 'this is My covenant with them: My Spirit who is upon you, and My words which I have put in your mouth, shall not depart from your mouth, nor from the mouth of your descendants, nor from the mouth of your descendants' descendants,' says the LORD, 'from this time and forevermore.'"[1] God is not saying here that He is going to lecture His children on the ABC's of doctrine. He is expressing that the full joy of the church will be found as His people are ruled by His Word and His Spirit—these two together. If we tear apart this union of Word and Spirit, we are guilty of a terrible sacrilege!

We should consider also that Paul was caught up to the third heaven, and yet he still studied the Law and the Prophets. He did not consider even such a profound experience to be any substitute for Scripture. He also urged Timothy to read, and he especially extolled Scripture as "profitable for doctrine, for reproof, for correction, for instruction in righteousness, that the man of God may be complete, thoroughly

---

[1] Isaiah 59:21

The Fantastic and Furious Sect of the Libertines

Calvin's response to most heretical teaching was firm but moderately charitable. Calvin freely acknowledged that all mankind is subject to error, and he urged believers to keep the Scripture always before their eyes so that their hearts would not be led away from the simplicity of the gospel.

When it came to the **Libertines**, however, Calvin pulled no punches. Galled by the gross perversion of the sect, Calvin could scarcely believe that serious Christians would pay attention to them at all. He was dismayed to see the Libertines gaining converts, and he felt compelled at last to confront them. In 1544, he wrote a treatise *Against the Fantastic and Furious Sect of the Libertines Who are Called 'Spirituals.'* He began his treatise with this bold statement: "Although all heretical sects are mortal pests in Christianity, nevertheless we do not read anywhere in all the early histories where there was ever a sect as pernicious as that which is today called the Libertines. Not only is it malicious, but it is so monstrous and churlish that there is not a man of sane judgment who can think of it without feeling horror."[1]

Although Calvin never named the group to which he referred in Chapter 9 of *The Institutes*, it is obviously none other than these same Libertines.

The Libertines believed that salvation by grace meant freedom from any moral or civil law. They openly indulged in sexual promiscuity and other gross sin. Whenever anyone challenged them from Scripture, they replied that Scripture was "dead letter" and did not apply to them. They placed heavy emphasis on personal revelation—dreams, visions, and prophecy.

Calvin had a dramatic show-down with Libertines in 1553. A wealthy Libertine named Philibert Berthelier was denied communion by the church, but he appealed to the city council and won his case. Calvin was ordered to serve the Lord's Supper to him. On the following Sunday, when the prayers were offered and the elements ready to be distributed, the Libertines rushed toward the table. Calvin flung his arms around the bread and wine and shouted, "These hands you may crush, these arms you may lop off, my life you may take, my blood is yours, you may shed it; but you shall never force me to give holy things to the profaned, and dishonor the table of my God."

Following this incident, Berthelier again applied for the right to take the Lord's Supper, but the city council ruled that the church courts had final say in the matter.

equipped for every good work."[2] It would be insanity to imagine that the Scriptures, which guide us to completion and equip us for every good work, would be some temporary thing which we no longer need!

Again, I would really like to ask these crazy people whether they have another spirit than the Spirit of Christ. Jesus promised to send One who did not speak on His own authority, but rather speaks what has already been said in the

---

[1] Calvin, John. *Treatises Against the Anabaptists and the Libertines.* Trans. Benjamin Wirt Farley. Baker Book House, 1982.

[2] II Timothy 3:16-17

John Calvin refused to serve communion to the Libertines.

Word.[1] It is not the work of the Holy Spirit to introduce new revelation or make up new teaching. The Holy Spirit illuminates the gospel which we have already heard so that we may understand it.

The Spirit Agrees With Scripture

From what we know of the Holy Spirit, we must recognize that we are commanded to diligently read and obey Scripture if we want to gain anything from the Spirit. We cannot expect the Holy Spirit to act apart from the Word. Furthermore, any spirit which bypasses the Bible and suggests another doctrine should be immediately recognized as a false, deceptive spirit. After all, we know

---

[1] John 16:13

Satan can appear as an angel of light.[1] How would we be able to tell which is the real Holy Spirit unless we had some means of differentiating true from false? Scripture is that mark by which we can know the true work of the Spirit.

Alarmingly, this reckless group pays no attention to warnings. They seek the Spirit within themselves rather than from God. Try to reason with them! Try to tell them that the Holy Spirit would not act against the Word! These foolish people merely sneer, "Don't put God in a box!" How is it "putting God in a box" to say that He would be consistent with Himself? Yes, it would be wrong to say that Spirit should be limited by human rules or in any other manner which would be outside Himself, but the Bible is the Word of God. How is it insulting the Holy Spirit to say that God's Word is what we expect God to say? I will admit that this is a test, and those of the heretical group would say that we should not test God. It is true that we should not *invent* tests for God. However, this test which I set out for them here is the very test God has authorized so that we may recognize Him, so that we may know truth from deception.

Let us settle the matter by acknowledging that God is always the same God. To think that He would speak in a manner inconsistent with Himself is absurd. It would be as if God turned against Himself and rebelled against His own kingdom.

The Union of Word and Spirit

This heretical group criticizes us for our insistence upon having Scripture as our foundation. They love to quote Paul's statement that the letter kills.[2] However, we must view that Bible verse in context. It is obvious that Paul was addressing false apostles who were setting forth the Law without Christ and drawing people away from the benefits of the new covenant. Without Christ's grace, the Law does kill. If God's Law is only heard with the ears and does not touch the heart, then it is death. However, if the Spirit engraves the Law upon the heart to show forth Christ, then it is life.

It is also noteworthy that in the very same chapter in which Paul speaks of the letter that kills, he also calls his preaching a "ministry of the Spirit."[3] He meant by this that the Spirit would never act apart from the Word. Only when proper reverence is shown for the Word does the Holy Spirit manifest His power, and only by the illumination of the Spirit can we put our faith in the Word. The Lord has put

---

[1] II Corinthians 11:14

[2] II Corinthians 3:6

[3] II Corinthians 3:8

a sort of mutual bond between His Word and His Spirit. We can only truly understand God's Word when the Holy Spirit shines in our hearts, and we can only be certain that the Spirit we follow is the Holy Spirit when we recognize Him in the Word.

God's Word is not a temporary phenomenon. The Holy Spirit did not come to *replace* the Word of God. The Holy Spirit *confirms* the Word of God. The Bible was given to us by the power of the Holy Spirit, and the Holy Spirit completes His work by illuminating the Word in our hearts.

When Jesus taught the disciples on the road to Emmaus, He urged them to remember the Scriptures rather than search their own thoughts and ideas.[1] Also, the apostle Paul, even as he taught the Thessalonians that they should not quench the Spirit, immediately added that they should not despise prophecy (God's Word).[2] Paul did not ramble off into speculation about the spirit world, as this heretical group always does. As soon as the Word of God is despised, the light of the Spirit also vanishes.

I am baffled by the foolish pride of these fanatics. They carelessly toss away the Word of God, and they put all their confidence in whatever crazy notion drifts into their dreams while they are snoring. As children of God, let us have nothing to do with this silliness. We know that the Holy Spirit shines the light of truth upon us. Likewise, we know that Scripture is the means by which God grants the light of His Spirit to believers. There is only one Spirit—He who indwelled the apostles and who still reminds us today to listen to the Word of God.

---

[1] Luke 24:27

[2] I Thessalonians 5:19-20

CHAPTER 10
SCRIPTURE TEACHES US TO WORSHIP GOD ALONE

God the Creator in Scripture

I have previously said that the knowledge of God shines forth most clearly in Scripture (although it is evident everywhere in creation). Now I shall begin a comparison of the revelation of God in Scripture and the revelation of God in nature. I could speak at great length on this subject, but I will restrict myself to those things which are most important to our discussion. I am also not yet going to address the subject of the covenant in which God chose Abraham and his children out of the other nations, since this will be covered in the next book. Even though it would lend a little to this discussion, I do not want to overlap too much with topics which will be covered in depth later.

At present, I will confine my writing to an investigation of God's role as Creator and King of the universe. Scripture repeatedly speaks of God's goodness and His fatherly kindness toward us. It also shows us His judgment; He punishes evil, especially when patience has proven futile.

A Comparison of the Attributes of God in Scripture and in Creation

Certain passages of the Bible reveal the character of God with particular clarity. One of these is found in Exodus 34 when Moses describes his encounter with God on Mount Sinai. God proclaims everything about His character which mankind is permitted to know: "The LORD, the LORD God, merciful and gracious, longsuffering, and abounding in goodness and truth, keeping mercy for thousands, forgiving iniquity and transgression and sin, by no means clearing the guilty, visiting the iniquity of the fathers upon the children and the children's children to the third and the fourth generation."[1]

---

[1] Exodus 34:6-7

God twice repeats His name "Jehovah" (translated "the LORD"), emphasizing His eternal nature. Then He lists attributes of Himself. Notice that these attributes are not theoretical or ethereal, but rather, they reveal His attitude toward us: kind, good, merciful, and just. These same attributes of God are revealed in the universe around us.

The prophets use similar words to describe God. We cannot go through all examples, but there are many, including a psalm listing God's attributes almost exactly as Moses did.[1] It is worth noting, however, that all these attributes of God can be seen in nature as well. Our own life experience teaches us that God is just and merciful, as the Bible also teaches us.

In the book of Jeremiah, God tells us again the things which He would have us know about Himself: "'But let him who glories glory in this, that he understands and knows Me, that I am the LORD, exercising lovingkindness, judgment, and righteousness in the earth. For in these I delight,' says the LORD."[2]

These are the things which God has determined most important for us to know about Him: His mercy (on which we all depend for our salvation), His judgment (which is every day carried out against evildoers and will be carried to more completion hereafter), and His justice (which tenderly rewards the righteous).

When we understand these three aspects of God's character, we cannot cease glorifying God. Of course, we are not neglecting God's other attributes— truth, power, holiness, and goodness. How could we even be certain of God's mercy or His justice unless we already believed in the unfailing truth of His Word? How could we trust in His justice unless we already knew that He rules over the earth in sovereign power? How could we believe Him to be merciful unless we knew Him to be good? And finally, when we see God's mercy, judgment, and justice together, then we see His holiness in all of these.

The knowledge of God learned from the Scriptures is the same which we might glean from His creation. The Bible carries the imprint of the same Person whose image is reflected also in His creatures. Our first goal should be to learn reverence of God and then secondly

---

History Corner

Justin Martyr (103 – 165 AD) was an early Christian teacher and writer. His parents were pagans, and Justin tried many philosophical paths prior to his conversion. He was influenced to become a Christian by witnessing the valor of Christians who were executed for their faith.

Justin faced his own martyrdom under the reign of Marcus Aurelius. He was beheaded in 165 AD.

---

[1] Psalm 145
[2] Jeremiah 9:24

to trust Him. Ultimately, we must learn to worship Him with sincere obedience and to lean upon His mercy.

The Inexcusable Worship of Idols

In summary, let me reiterate that the Bible directs us to the true God and forcefully rejects all pagan gods. Religion has been polluted throughout human history, and yet, mankind has never entirely lacked the concept of one God. People might worship a whole army of gods, but then they suddenly revert to speaking simply of "God" whenever they are discussing true nature. Justin Martyr noted this in his book *On the Monarchy of God*, in which he pointed out many examples which together prove that there is some understanding of God's oneness naturally imprinted upon the human heart.

Despite all this, mankind does not have the ability to make any proper use of their instinctive understanding of God's nature. Even the wisest pagans wandered vaguely among many concepts of "God" in their prayers and petitions. Uneducated people fared even worse with their veneration of Jupiter, Mercury, Venus, Minerva, and so on. God engraves His truth on the heart of each person, but His truth is corrupted by each person as well.

This tendency to always slide away from the truth of God is the reason that the prophet Habakkuk condemned all idols and urged everyone to seek God in His Temple.[1] Only through the instruction of the Word of God can believers be certain that they worship the true God rather than their own corrupt fantasy.

---

[1] Habakkuk 2:20

CHAPTER 11
NO GRAVEN IMAGES

No Pictures or Statues of God

Scripture takes into account the foolishness of mankind when it repeatedly contrasts the true worship of God with the worship of idols. I do not mean to minimize other false forms of worship which might be more subtle (such as some forms endorsed by pagan philosophers), but the insanity of idolatry is particularly prevalent in the human heart. While ostensibly searching for God, each person clings to his or her own particular idea of God. If we are honest, we must admit that there can only be one true character of God. It does not particularly matter whether this person thinks one thing or that person thinks another thing about God. God Himself declares who He is, and His definition is the only one that matters.

Such stupidity has seized the entire world that mankind has everywhere sought to make God visible in the form of wood, stone, gold, silver, or other materials which decay and rust. True believers must realize that God's glory is degraded whenever someone tries to represent Him through a picture or a statue.

In the Ten Commandments, God first proclaims that all glory belongs to Himself, and then He immediately adds, "You shall not make for yourself a carved image—any likeness of anything that is in heaven above, or that is in the earth beneath, or that is in the water under the earth."[1] With this statement, He curbs our natural impulse to represent Him with a visible image of something around us. The Persians worshiped the sun, other pagans worshiped the stars, the Egyptians fashioned gods resembling all manner of animals, and the Greeks (perhaps the wisest in their choice) carved human images to represent their gods. However, in giving His Law, God does not even distinguish between one sort of representation and another. He simply condemns all pictures, statues, or other visible forms through which foolish people may attempt to draw near to Him.

---

[1] Exodus 20:4

Idols, Idols Everywhere

Calvin defines an idol as anything taking the place of God and receiving the honor due Him. Pagans had idols aplenty, and yet we who claim to shun idolatry are often no better in our distracted worship. Our hearts turn away from the pure worship of God to seek out something more comfortable and familiar. Pagans set up false images of God in their temples; we set up false images of God in our hearts.

It is a very short step from imagining a new god to creating a physical idol, and Christians who begin the process tend to continue the downhill slide. "The mind envisions it, and the hand creates it," Calvin says. Those who accept images in churches may attempt to excuse their sin by claiming that they are not worshiping an image exactly, but merely adoring it, or some similar wordplay. These weak excuses only prove that they realize they are doing wrong by setting up an image in a place of worship at all.

Calvin's primary target in this discussion was Catholicism. Roman Catholic churches overflowed with statues of Jesus, Mary, and the saints. Calvin's position on use of images was simple and radical: all statues or pictures used as a focus of worship are idols, and all idols must be destroyed.

Graven Images Invariably Deny God's True Nature

God gives us reasons for His prohibition of graven images. In Deuteronomy, He declares through Moses, "Take careful heed to yourselves, for you saw no form when the LORD spoke to you at Horeb out of the midst of the fire, lest you act corruptly and make for yourselves a carved image in the form of any figure: the likeness of male or female."[1] When we see how plainly God speaks against all visual representations of Himself, we may be sure that anyone who makes an image of God does so in disobedience to God's express command. All graven images distort God's true nature.

The prophet Isaiah emphatically opposes visual representations of God.[2] Isaiah teaches that God's glory is dishonored by these silly fabrications. How can God – the infinite and eternal Spirit – be reduced in likeness to a feeble bit of wood or stone or gold? The apostle Paul makes the same point: "Therefore, since we are the offspring of God, we ought not to think that the Divine Nature is like gold or silver or stone, something shaped by art and man's devising."[3] God clearly reveals that He is displeased with any image set up to represent Him.

---

[1] Deuteronomy 4:15-16
[2] Isaiah 40:18-20, 46:5-7
[3] Acts 17:29

The Ark of the Covenant

People who defend the use of images in worship often hinge their case upon a particular feature of Old Testament worship. In the book of Exodus, God commanded the Israelites to build the Ark of the Covenant. Positioned on top of the Ark was the mercy seat, the place where God's glory dwelled.

God ordered the construction of the mercy seat to include images: "And you shall make two cherubim of gold; of hammered work you shall make them at the two ends of the mercy seat."

Calvin notes that his opponents fail to mention the other instructions regarding the cherubim: "And the cherubim shall stretch out their wings above, covering the mercy seat with their wings, and they shall face one another; the faces of the cherubim shall be toward the mercy seat... And there I will meet with you, and I will speak with you from above the mercy seat, from between the two cherubim which are on the ark of the Testimony, about everything which I will give you in commandment to the children of Israel."[1]

Calvin argues that God positioned the cherubim very carefully in order to strongly discourage any inclination to worship them. These angel figures were not intended to represent God. Furthermore, the cherubim faced each other, not the worshiper, and God spoke from the empty space between them. Finally, the entire ark was placed behind a heavy veil, out of sight of the people of Israel during worship.

The Holy Spirit's thunderous command forbidding the worship of graven images reaches even worshipers of pagan idols. Augustine quotes Seneca's complaint: "They make the holy eternal gods out of the most dishonorable substance, and they carve them in the form of men and animals. Some of them are given bizarre characteristics and gender-confused bodies. And these are supposedly gods, although, if they ever actually came alive and stood before us, we would think that they were monsters."[2]

When we take all of this evidence together, it is obvious that God's prohibition of graven images applies just as much to us now as it ever did to anyone. Some people today claim that such a rule was intended only for the Jews because of their tendency toward superstition in that era, but those who say this are dodging the real issue. God's declaration of His nature is eternal – for everyone forever. And, as a side note, Paul was speaking to the Athenians (not the Jews) when he said that we should not think that the Divine Nature is like gold or silver or stone.

---

[1] Exodus 25:20-22

[2] Augustine, *City of God*, Chapter 10.

Statues and Pictures of God Are Forbidden in Scripture

From time to time, God has revealed His presence in a certain definite and visible manner. The Bible speaks of seeing God *face-to-face*. However, when we examine these examples carefully, we see that each occasion still conveys to us the same sense of awe at God's unfathomable nature. God appeared to the Israelites as a pillar of cloud or a fire, glorious and yet beyond human understanding.[1] Moses pleaded to see the face of God, but he was told that no one could look upon the face of God and live.[2] The Holy Spirit descended on Christ in form of a dove, but that particular symbol lasted only for a moment and then vanished forever. [3] After that, believers were taught to trust in the invisible Spirit and to be content with His power and grace. On several occasions in the Old Testament, God appeared in human form (foreshadowing the incarnation of Christ), but this was never considered an excuse to carve an image of God in human form.

Finally, let us consider the Ark of the Covenant. Two statues of cherubim stood on either side of the mercy seat, and some people have argued that this proves the acceptability of images in worship. However, the careful design of this feature on the Ark of the Covenant strongly discouraged any focus on the images themselves and lifted the minds of the worshipers instead toward reverence of God. The cherubim were placed so that their outspread wings covered the mercy seat, and the Ark of the Covenant itself was hidden behind a veil.[4] The little angel images were never intended to *represent* God; their entire purpose was to shroud the manifestation of God from human eyes. Furthermore, you will notice that when the prophets describe their visions, they speak of the angels appearing with their faces covered.[5] God's glory shines in such brilliance that even the angels cannot look directly upon it, and even the glimmers of His glory in the faces of the angels are hidden from human eyes. Ultimately, all of these things – the mercy seat, the images of the cherubim, and so forth – are from a bygone era. It is silly to bring them up as if we are to duplicate them in our worship of God today.

The psalmist declares, "The idols of the nations are silver and gold, the work of men's hands."[6] In that brief statement, several things are abundantly clear:

---

[1] Exodus 13:21
[2] Exodus 33:20
[3] Matthew 3:16
[4] Exodus 25:17-21
[5] Isaiah 6:2
[6] Psalm 135:15

graven images are not true gods, any representation of God dreamed up by a human is false, and expensive materials (gold, silver, etc.) do not improve the situation. A visual representation of God – whether made from wood and clay or from gold and silver – diminishes the glory of God.

Humans are swept away by arrogance and foolishness when they worship something made by their own hands. There is much truth contained in the mocking poem:

> *I was once a fig-tree's trunk, a lump of useless wood,*
> *Till the carpenter, uncertain whether to*
> *carve Priapus*
> *Or a stool, decided on the god.*[1]

As the poem indicates, there is something absurd in the notion that man (who is so mortal that every breath brings him a little closer to the grave) can make an eternal god from a dead piece of wood. However, I am reluctant to praise the writings of the Epicureans in their mockery of all things religious, and so let us take our lesson from the prophets instead. Isaiah speaks of the foolishness of those people who use part of a piece of wood to cook their dinner and the other part to make a god and then bow before their wooden god and pray.[2] Isaiah scolds them not only for breaking the law, but also for violating common sense about the manner in which the earth was founded.[3] How can we imagine that the immortal and infinite God could be reduced to a five-foot statue? Nevertheless, this ridiculous idea is all too common among humankind. Idolatry is everywhere.

Scripture plainly rebukes all who use images in worship. Without exception, visual representations of God are described in the Bible as "the work of men's hands,"[4] emphasizing that these things are not authorized by God. The psalmist lashes out angrily at idolaters who should be smart enough to know better; everyone

---

Ancient Philosopher Roll Call

The poem referenced by Calvin in this chapter was written by Roman philosopher and poet **Quintus Horatius Flaccus** (65 BC – 8 BC), commonly known as **Horace**.

Horace was an Epicurean. His collection of poems called *The Satires* (from which Calvin quotes in this chapter) mocks religion and ambition, while praising self-sufficiency and moderation as the keys to happiness.

---

[1] Horace, *The Satires*, "Once I Was a Fig-Tree Trunk." Trans. by A.S. Kline

[2] Isaiah 44:9-20

[3] Isaiah 40:21

[4] Psalm 135:15, Isaiah 2:8, Isaiah 37:19, Micah 5:13, and more

can see that all things move by the power of God and not by the word of lifeless, inanimate objects. The seriousness of this error is such that the Spirit breathes out a grim warning against idolaters: "Those who make them are like them; so is everyone who trusts in them."[1]

Before I conclude this section, I should add that the commandment forbids making *any likeness* of God. Let us not get sidetracked by the foolish nitpicking of the Greek Orthodox Church. They claim that this rule does not apply to them because they use pictures instead of statues. Yet everything said about graven images applies to pictures as well. God forbids both statues and pictures, and any other likeness of Himself that mankind may dream up. The glory of God cannot be reduced to a picture any more than it can be reduced to a statue.

Pope Gregory's Big Mistake

There is a tiresome old saying going around which claims that images are like books for those who cannot read. Gregory has said this, but the Holy Spirit has said otherwise. If Gregory himself were properly educated in the Word of God, he would never have said such a thing.

> **"Perhaps God was merely expressing a preference for paint!"**
>
> Greek Orthodox churches are well-known for their use of icons in worship.
> These icons are two-dimensional paintings purportedly representing Christ or one of the saints. Icons are frequently used as objects of reverence and prayer.
> Many people in the Greek Orthodox Church believe that they cannot be accused of idolatry because they venerate pictures. They claim that only statues can be idols.

Jeremiah declares that everyone taught by idols is dull-hearted and foolish; Habakkuk proclaims that images teach only lies.[2] Whatever teaching anyone might gain from an idol is worthless and misleading. Some people would argue that the prophets were speaking to a special case in which images were being used in a false and misleading manner. Certainly, those images were being used to deceive, but I reply that this is the case for *all* images which are purported to represent God. The prophets do not differentiate between "good idols" and "bad idols." All idols are equally condemned. The prophets only distinguish between idols and the true God, and they make it abundantly clear that those two never overlap. *All* graven images are deceitful, and *all* who worship them are deluded. Therefore, *all* knowledge of God drawn from graven images is corrupt. When I say this, I am merely repeating almost word for word what the Bible says about it.

---

[1] Psalm 115:8

[2] Jeremiah 10:8, Habakkuk 2:18

The Roman Catholic Church should be ashamed of their ducking and dodging on this subject, especially their claim that images are books for the poorly educated. This is simply rebellion against Scripture. Even supposing that I granted them this point and did not argue it, where would that get them? They set these obscene eyesores out to represent God and the saints. There are statues of the Virgin Mary portraying her in clothes that would embarrass a prostitute. I would beg the Catholic Church to minimally put in enough effort to dress their idols appropriately. With that done, perhaps the Catholics would not sound quite so ridiculous when they claim that these images teach the common people about holiness.

The truth is that the Roman Catholicism has grown lazy. Rather than bothering to actually teach anyone, they set up these images and consider their job done. Who are these people the Catholic Church dismisses as uneducated? They are God's elect. The Lord called them to be His disciples and honored them with the revelation of Himself. It is the will of God that His people should be properly taught about salvation, sanctification, and all other matters of His Kingdom. I agree that there are many people today who could not get by in worship without their "books" (idols). They have been cheated by those who were supposed to instruct them. Many church leaders are so incompetent that they have nothing to say about God, and so they turn their crucial responsibility over to idols and declare those idols to be teachers of the ignorant.

The apostle Paul tells us that it is by the *preaching of the gospel* that Christ crucified is portrayed to us.[1] If this is how we are to see the crucified Lord, then why

---

[1] Galatians 3:1

all these crucifixes of wood, stone, silver, and gold? When the congregation is faithfully taught, they have no need for these things. We must tell people plainly that Christ died on the cross to bear our curse, that He sacrificed His own body to pay for our sins, that He washed our sins away with His own blood, and that we have been reconciled to God the Father. From this one simple statement, they can learn more than they ever could from a thousand crucifixes of wood or stone. Only greedy people would rather stare at gold and silver than hear the Word of God.

Origins of Idolatry

The human heart is filled with self-centered arrogance, and so there is a tendency within us to imagine a god that is more like ourselves or, at least, something which we may easily understand. People then turn to express whatever god they have dreamed up, and a new idol is born – the mind envisions it, and the hand creates it. Why create it? We fashion these images because our spiritual blindness leads us to believe that God is not with us unless He is there in some physically obvious way.

We see this aspect of human nature in the story of the Israelites demanding that Aaron make them an idol to worship. They said, "Come, make us gods that shall go before us; for as for this Moses, the man who brought us up out of the land of Egypt, we do not know what has become of him."[1] These people had experienced the mighty power of God through the working of great miracles, and yet, the moment the physical representative of God was out of sight, they felt abandoned and wished for something to stand before them as proof of God's presence. Human nature is always nervous until it finds something physical like itself to use as an image of God. Idolatry infiltrates every era of human history as people search for something to fill the apparent void.

When people do settle on something as a physical representation of God, worship of that thing follows immediately. People may tell themselves initially that the thing they have set up is only a reminder of the presence of God. Yet, once the eyes and hearts are fixed upon a material image, people inevitably conclude that the thing itself contains some divine power.

Dear reader, if you bow down to honor an image, you are already trapped in a terrible superstition. There is no substantive difference between worshiping God represented in an image and worshiping an idol. Humans are too stupid to enforce that fine distinction in their worship. As soon as something seems to represent God,

---

[1] Exodus 32:1

they immediately believe that it has the power of God. It is impossible for them to "adore" without worshiping. Since God is displeased with any form of superstitious worship, honor given to an image is honor stolen from Him.

As for those people who emphasize the supposed distinction between worshiping an idol and worshiping God through an idol, I have one more thing to say to them. The Israelites were not so careless that they forgot who had brought them out of Egypt, even when they made the golden calf. When Aaron presented the calf to the people, he proclaimed that it was the same God who had led them out of Egypt, and the people boldly agreed. They were not trying to abandon the God who had liberated them; they merely wished to see Him leading them in the form of a golden calf. Furthermore, even the pagans were not so stupid that they really believed that God was made of wood and stone. They had thousands of images of the same god or goddess. They changed images whenever they pleased, but they always kept the same deity in mind. They even consecrated new idols every day, but they did not think they were accumulating new gods. Augustine recounts the objections of the heathens of his day when they were accused of worshiping unconscious statues: they replied that they did not worship the statue itself but an invisible deity residing there.

Idolatry is idolatry, whether it occurs among the Israelites (as when they bowed before the golden calf) or among the pagans and their various false gods. It springs from the same root: a discontented attitude toward the spiritual nature of God and a grasping for a physical representation of Him. As soon as the ball commences rolling in that direction, there is no stopping it. Whatever good intentions may have existed at the beginning, the end certainly will be that the worshipers suppose that the power of God resides in an image.

Images and Art in the Church

I am amazed that some people still brazenly argue that there is no worship of images going on in the Roman Catholic Church. Anyone can see that this is a lie. Why do people kneel before the images? Why do people pray to the images as if they are speaking to God? Certainly, Augustine spoke truly that anyone who gazes at a picture or statue while praying will eventually be influenced to believe that the image is listening to him.[1] If there is no worship of these images, then why do

---

[1] Augustine, *Psalms*, Psalm 115.

people take pilgrimages to see them even when they have copies of them at home? Why are they willing to take up the sword to defend the images even if it means brutal violence and bloodshed? It seems that many people can more easily bear the thought of eternal separation from the true God than the idea of losing their beloved idols.

Perhaps the multitude today will not admit to idolatry or call the images "gods" (and I daresay the ancient Israelites would react the same way about their idolatry), but the prophets never hesitated to call idolatry by its real name. God's prophets openly proclaimed that Israel was being unfaithful to God by showing honor to idols. The prophets would say the same to the church today. We must do away with idolatrous worship.

Having said all of that, I must add that I am not so gripped by superstition that I think all images everywhere must be destroyed. Painting and sculpture are gifts of God. These gifts should be used properly for the glory of God and for our own good. We must not permit talent to be twisted for corrupt purposes. We believe that it is wrong to represent God with a graven image because God Himself has forbidden it and because it dishonors His glory. We are not alone in holding this view; competent theologians throughout Christian history have disapproved of representing God with pictures and statues. It is not right to make an image of God at all, and it is far worse to worship it or (as some may phrase it) to worship God through it. Since creating images of God is forbidden, sculpture and painting should be limited to those things which are visible to us. God is beyond human visual perception.

> ## Support the Arts!
>
> Calvin clarifies that he is not opposed to art for purely decorative or educational purposes. In fact, he declares that painting and sculpture are gifts from God.

Of course, many religious statues and pictures in churches today were never intended to represent God. These images serve very little purpose at all. A few may depict historical events, but most exist merely for decoration. Because they were chosen strictly on the basis of the pleasure they inspire in the viewer, most of them were not wisely selected. I have noted that some of these statues are embarrassingly immodest. I suppose a case could be made that such artwork is not necessarily evil, but it is definitely not helpful either.

I have no inclination to speak much about distinctions between appropriate and inappropriate images. I think it would be wiser to question whether it is a good idea to have statues and pictures in a church at all. If we have any respect for the early church, we should remember that it carried on very well for five hundred years without the assistance of images. Only when the purity of the church became more compromised did statues and pictures become commonplace as church decoration. I am not going to delve into all the history behind the introduction of images into churches, but if you compare the early era to the later era, it is obvious that these changes were symptoms of declining integrity.

If pictures and statues were as useful as many today claim, why would the early church fathers persist so long in worshiping without them? Clearly, those early believers saw no usefulness in images, or else they saw a little use but also much danger. The lack of images in the early church was not a mere oversight; it was quite deliberate. Augustine says about images in churches: "When they are lifted up to places of honor and served by those who pray and sacrifice, then the similarity that they bear to human form has a strange effect on the weak-minded. Although the images do not have any consciousness or life, some people behave as though the image is alive."[1] In another writing, he adds, "The shape of the idol's body is enough like our own to trick the human mind into supposing that the idol has feelings."[2] And later, he continues, "Images have more power to warp the troubled soul than to mend it, because although the image has a mouth, eyes, ears, and feet, it does not speak, see, hear, or walk."[3]

Perhaps confusion between the appearance and the reality is the reason John warned us not only against worshiping idols, but even against the idols themselves.[4] In these crazy days in which godliness seems almost blotted out, we have witnessed far too much of the evil influence of idolatry. We cannot dismiss it as a trivial problem. The foolishness of human nature flings people directly into superstition as soon as it can gain a foothold.

Even if we were not living in such dangerous times, I would question the appropriateness of images of any kind in a church. Consider the intended purpose of a church, and whether it is proper to have in a sacred place any symbol other than those which God Himself has provided for us in His Word (I mean, of course, baptism and the Lord's Supper). Other pictures are all man-made and can only distract from those things which God would prefer that we contemplate during a worship service.

---

[1] Augustine, *Letters*, 102

[2] Augustine, *City of God*, Chapter 4

[3] Augustine, *Psalms*, Psalm 115

[4] I John 5:21

CHAPTER 12
THE SUPREME AND ONLY GOD

The One and Only God

I have said from the beginning of this book that our knowledge of God does not depend upon vague theorizing about the existence of God, but rather, it includes devotion and obedience to God. We have briefly discussed the proper worship of God, and I will discuss that more in time. For now, I will briefly reiterate that the Bible proclaims that there is only one God. In making this exclusive statement, the Scriptures are not merely quibbling over the proper name of God, but rather they are declaring that we must never ascribe to any other the honor which is due God alone.

The difference between true Christianity and all other religions centers upon exactly whom we worship and how. Even pagans recognize some necessity of adhering to a proper form of worship. The Greek word for "religion" also has a connotation of appropriate reverence (as contrasted to lawlessness). Godliness is well-established and secure only when it is restrained within appropriate boundaries. Superstition occurs whenever people are not content to worship God in the manner in which He has directed us to worship Him. When people cast aside proper order, they pile up one meaningless absurdity after another.

Consider also that people have always understood the possibility that true religion may be corrupted through error and false teaching. If something can be corrupted, it must first have a correct way. Therefore, if we cast aside the proper form and give in to whatever zeal seizes us at the moment, we are behaving senselessly. Everyone knows this, and yet everyone wants to worship God however they please. God does not permit this. He declares that He is a jealous God who punishes those who fail to properly distinguish between Him and other gods.[1] God decides which forms of worship are lawful, and He commands obedience. One reason for this is to restrain mankind from drifting into savage rituals. Regardless of

---

[1] Exodus 20:5

all the reasons surrounding this principle, I will say again as I have said before: all proper reverence is that which is given to God in the manner He has set down as appropriate. Anything else robs God of the honor due Him.

Veneration of Saints

We must pay very careful attention to subtle deception. Error can be insidious. Superstition slips into worship when God is permitted to remain at the highest place but He is surrounded by a crowd of lesser gods who are supposed to act on His behalf. God's glory is torn apart piece by piece in this deception, subtly and quietly. This error has plagued the worship of God throughout history. Recently, it has found its way into the church through the veneration of deceased saints. Many people imagine that these saints are involved in a sort of partnership with God. They even pray to saints as they would pray to God. This abominable practice retains a bare acknowledgment of God's superiority, but turns hearts away from Him and toward the worship of false gods.

Those who venerate saints attempt to draw some distinction between the worship given to God and the honor bestowed upon the dead (or upon angels, as the case may be). There is no practical difference between the devotion people bestow on the saints and the devotion they give to God. Only when they are cornered about it do people begin to squirm uncomfortably and try to make some verbal distinction between "latria" and "dulia," and they claim that their "dulia" is all perfectly acceptable because they keep all the "latria" for God. What do words matter? It is the thing itself which is the issue, not the particular term used to describe it. This wordplay is absurd. Wrong does not become right simply because a new label is attached to it.

God reserves *all* worship for Himself alone. We dishonor God whenever we take that which is due Him and distribute it among a crowd of lesser gods or dead heroes.

Word Games

Calvin accuses the Catholic Church of playing silly word games in their attempt to justify their idolatry. Roman Catholic theologians attempt to distinguish between **latria** (reverence toward God) and **dulia** (reverence toward saints). Latria is viewed as a higher and deeper veneration, while dulia is an expression of admiration and respect considered proper to heroes of the faith.

Calvin, however, dismisses this as "wordplay." Whatever excuses may be offered for it, he could find no practical difference between the practices involved in veneration of the saints and those used in the worship of God.

CHAPTER 13
TRINITY

God is an Immeasurable Spirit

The Bible teaches us that God is an infinite Spirit. Today there are many misconceptions concerning the essence of God, just as there were many errors among the ancient philosophers also. One such philosopher said, "Whatever we see, and whatever we do not see, is God."[1] (He imagined that God's divine essence was poured into every part of the world.) God Himself says relatively little about His essence, but what He does say is enough to drive out many stupid fantasies of the human mind.

Once we understand that God is truly infinite, we see the futility of any attempt to measure Him by human assessment. If we comprehend that God is Spirit, we must realize that there is nothing fleshly about Him. To clarify this even more to us, God describes the heavens as His dwelling place. Of course, He fills the whole earth as well, but He emphasizes the heavens because we are creatures of the earth with sluggish, downward-drifting minds. God raises our thoughts toward heaven.

---

[1] Seneca, *Natural Questions*, Book I, Chapter XIII.

Ancient Philosopher Roll Call

Calvin's allusion to "one such philosopher" is a reference to **Lucius Annaeus Seneca** (c. 4 – 65 AD), also known as **Seneca the Younger.** Seneca was a Roman Stoic philosopher and statesman. As a Stoic, Seneca believed that everything in the universe was composed of a combination of matter and "God," defined as an intelligent force of fate.

Seneca was so highly regarded by the church in the Middle Ages that it was rumored that he had been converted to Christianity by the apostle Paul, but there is no historical evidence to support this. Calvin certainly had no admiration for Seneca's view of God as a fatalistic force infusing everything. Calvin declared that Stoicism (like other pagan concepts of God) resulted from vain human imagination.

> **"But how can God see me if I hide behind a tree?"**
>
> The **Anthropomorphites** referred to in this chapter were a Christian sect which arose in the fourth century. Their founder, Audius, taught that the Bible should be taken literally when it speaks of God's body parts, and so God must have a human form. Anthropomorphites viewed God as a powerful giant rather than a Spirit. Such a limited view of God quickly led to even more heresy, including a denial of God's omnipresence, since it would be impossible for a being with a human body to be everywhere. Theologians of that era quickly dismissed this bizarre notion of God's nature and attributed the error to extraordinary ignorance.
>
> Modern-day Anthropomorphites include the Church of Jesus Christ of Latter-Day Saints (Mormonism), which teaches that God has a physical body like a man.

This infinity of God's nature stands in direct contradiction to the teaching of the Manichees. They propose a sort of dualism in which God and Satan are nearly equal. Since God cannot be infinite if there is another being nearly equal in authority, the Manichees' view of God is very limited. Such ideas can only come from dreadful ignorance to the point of insanity.

> **Remember!**
>
> The **Manichees** were dualists who viewed the universe in terms of two opposing forces of spirit and matter engaged in a cosmic battle.

We may just as easily refute the childish teachings of the Anthropomorphites, who claim that God has a body, including mouth, ears, eyes, hands, and feet. They derive this idea, of course, from scriptural references which speak as if God possesses these body parts. How could anyone not understand that God uses a sort of baby-talk with us? We are like infants compared to Him; He knows our limited capacity. In His compassion, He comes down to our level to speak to us in words we can understand. These references to eyes and ears and hands were never intended to describe God's physical appearance.

One God, Three Persons

While God portrays Himself as the one and only God, He also describes Himself as three Persons. Unless we are able to lay hold of this truth, we will never have more than a vague impression of God. True knowledge requires that we have some understanding of the Trinity. I want to be very clear that I am not proposing that there are three Gods or that God splits apart somehow into three Persons. To ensure that nobody misunderstands me, I will spend some time discussing definitions.

Unfortunately, there are heretics among us who denounce our use of the terms "Trinity" and "Person" as unbiblical. Regardless of whether the actual words are found in Scripture, the concept is clearly present: there are three Persons spoken of, and each Person is fully God, and yet there is only one God. By introducing these words, we are only describing the plain teaching of Scripture on the subject. The words are used to clarify the concept, not to introduce any new or unscriptural idea.

Setting aside this debate over the use of terms, I will move on to discussing the definitions themselves. When I speak of a "Person" of the Trinity, I mean a *subsistence* in God's *essence* – each related to the other Persons, but also different. Consider John 1:1: "In the beginning was the Word, and the Word was with God, and the Word was God." If there were no distinctions between the Persons of the Trinity, then John could not say that the Word was *with* God. Yet, immediately after saying that the Word was with God, John declares the Word *was* God, thereby emphasizing the unity of God.

The three Persons of the Trinity are united so that they cannot be separated; they are one. However, each Person has qualities of His own that distinguish Him from the others, though they are all the same essence. The term "God" may apply to the Father, Son, or Holy Spirit (or all three together). There is unity of essence, but the Persons are also related to one another, and when we compare them we see that there are characteristics of the Father which do not apply to the Son, and there are characteristics of the Son which do not apply to the Holy Spirit.

On this topic, I will accept Tertullian's definition of the Trinity (if we understand it in the right way). Tertullian explains that there is a sort of internal arrangement that does not affect the complete unity of essence in God.

The Deity of Christ in the Old Testament

Before I go on, I must take some time to discuss the deity of the Son and the Holy Spirit. I am not yet going to address Christ's role as our Mediator, since we will discuss this in the next book. As we noted in the previous section, Jesus is the Word made flesh.

History Corner

Quintus Septimius Florens Tertullianus (c. 160 – c. 225 AD), also known as **Tertullian**, was a well-educated Roman who converted from paganism to Christianity in 198 AD. He was a prolific writer who produced more than forty works on a variety of theological topics.

Tertullian joined a sect of Montanists in 207 AD, and later separated from them to form a sect of his own. Tertullian is known for an unhealthy asceticism and a divisive nature.

However, his writings also include helpful treatises attacking heresy, defending Christianity against pagan prejudices, and explaining the Trinity.

Jehovah, Our Elohim ...

יְהוָה אֱלֹהֵינוּ

The Hebrew Scriptures use several different words to refer to God. The term **Elohim** is a generic term meaning simply "god," and it can be used to discuss either pagan gods or the one God worshiped by the Israelites, depending on the context.

The sacred name of God, however, is only ever used to speak of the one true God. Written as יהוה in Hebrew, this name has been alternately translated as Yahweh, Jehovah, or simply LORD (the capital letters indicating to the reader that the original text contains the sacred name of God). Jews and early Christians held this name of God so sacred that they never spoke it aloud. Even today, the word "Adonai" (Lord) is typically substituted for God's sacred name as a sign of respect whenever the Scriptures are read in Hebrew.

The two terms are often used together, as in Psalm 8: "O LORD, our Lord, how majestic is Your name in all the earth!" The two words for God consecutively read: "Jehovah, our Elohim..."

The mysterious Angel of the Lord who appears at various times in the Old Testament puts Jewish theologians in a quandary when He is described as "Elohim." The Jews attempt to circumvent this difficulty by claiming that "Elohim" could also be applied to mere angels, and thus, the Angel of the Lord should not be viewed as divine. Calvin argues that the word "Elohim" was never used for any except a deity. Furthermore, the sacred name of God is even applied to the Angel, which would be shocking blasphemy unless the Angel was indeed God Himself. The Angel could only have been a glimpse of Jesus Christ before the incarnation.

John declares that the Word was *God*. This is a very exclusive title. In Psalm 45:6, we read, "Your throne, O God, is forever and ever." Some Jewish scholars have claimed that this term "Elohim" (God) which is found in the psalm (and many other Bible passages) could apply to angels and other spiritual powers.

However, we find no justification for this view in Scripture. Nowhere in the Bible is an eternal throne provided for a mere creature. We never find a creature referred to as simply "God." In Exodus, the Lord told Moses that He had made him "as God to Pharaoh,"[1] but we note the all-important qualifier: "as." Moses was not actually God. Only Christ is said to be "God" with no qualifier.

More Old Testament evidence of Christ's divinity is found in the book of Isaiah: "His name will be called Wonderful, Counselor, Mighty God, Everlasting Father, Prince of Peace."[2] The Jews also try to avoid this verse by claiming an alternate translation. They say that it should read, "This is the name by which the

---

[1] Exodus 7:1

[2] Isaiah 9:6

Wonderful Counselor, Mighty God, and Everlasting Father will call him: the Prince of Peace." This idea does not make much practical sense, however. Considering the context is speaking of the coming Messiah, it seems obvious that the list of titles applies to Him. There would be no point in suddenly breaking away to list titles instead for God the Father.

Still clearer is the portion of Jeremiah which reads, "'Behold, the days are coming,' says the LORD, 'That I will raise to David a Branch of righteousness... Now this is His name by which He will be called: THE LORD OUR RIGHTEOUSNESS.'"[1] Jewish scholars may claim that other terms for God are titles which can apply to angels or other beings, but the name "Jehovah" (translated "the LORD") is universally viewed as belonging to God alone. We are forced to the conclude that the Son of God is the eternal God, the same God who declares that He will not give His glory to another.[2]

In reference to the Jewish confusion between God and angels, it should be noted that Jehovah is presented many times as an angel in the Old Testament. In several stories, this angel is said to have appeared, claiming for Himself the name of the eternal God. Some may try to dodge this problem by offering alternative explanations for the use of God's name, but the dilemma is not resolved so easily. A created angel would never permit a sacrifice to be offered to him rather than to God. Yet we see in Judges that an angel declined to eat bread, but instead directed Manoah and his wife to offer a sacrifice to Jehovah. Realizing the angel was Jehovah, Manoah cried out, "We shall surely die, because we have seen God!"[3]

Manoah's wife answered, "If the LORD had desired to kill us, He would not have accepted a burnt offering and a grain offering from our hands." Notice that (in the original language) she used the name Jehovah, the name of God.

The angel's reply removes any lingering doubts about His identity: "Why do you ask My name, seeing it is wonderful?"

The confusion of Jewish theologians on this matter is nothing compared to the impiety of Servetus. He claims that God never revealed Himself to Abraham and the other patriarchs at all, but that they were all worshiping an angel! However, the orthodox theologians of the church have always wisely interpreted these Old Testament verses to mean that the supreme Angel is, in fact, the Word—Christ Himself. We see the Angel act as Mediator in foretaste of things to come. Although

---

[1] Jeremiah 23:5-6

[2] Isaiah 42:8

[3] Judges 13

Michael Servetus: A Heretic in Geneva

MICHAEL SERVETVS ... DE ARAGONIA

Michael Servetus (1511-1553), a contemporary of John Calvin, is an extremely controversial figure in the history of the Protestant Reformation. Servetus lived in Spain during his early years where he was taught the Bible by Dominican friars. Servetus began to study law, but he was soon swept up in the Reformation.

Servetus developed a non-Trinitarian theology and began to widely publicize his views. Servetus taught that Jesus did not exist from all eternity but came into being at the incarnation. He rejected the title "Eternal Son of God" for Christ, preferring instead to refer to Jesus as "Son of the Eternal God." In an ill-fated attempt to persuade Calvin to support his theological ideas, Servetus drew him into an extended correspondence. Calvin makes reference to Servetus' absurd doctrine in this section of the *Institutes* (initially composed while Servetus was living and writing in France). Ultimately, Calvin ended the correspondence when it became clear that Servetus would not repent of teaching heresy. Servetus continued to write to Calvin and requested permission to see Calvin in Geneva, a request which Calvin steadfastly refused. Calvin threatened that Servetus would be captured if he presented himself there.

Servetus had, by this time, alienated himself from every part of Christendom. Catholics and Protestants alike were enraged by his writings, especially his comparison of the Trinity to Cerberus, a mythical three-headed dog. He was arrested for heresy in France and condemned to death, but he escaped from prison and set out for Italy. Ignoring Calvin's warnings, he stopped at Geneva and attended one of Calvin's sermons. He was promptly recognized and arrested by those present. Servetus was imprisoned for a time while the Geneva council sought advice from other cities concerning what to do with him. During his imprisonment, he wrote letters to the council calling for Calvin's arrest and execution. Eventually, he was brought to trial, condemned for heresy, and burned at the stake.

Calvin's role in the execution of Servetus is heavily disputed. Some refer to his prior warnings and his influence in Geneva and conclude that Calvin was personally and primarily responsible for Servetus' death. Others point out that Calvin was in ill health at the time and did not even appear at the trial, and that the trial was a civil matter in which Calvin was not even permitted to vote. It is known that Calvin did provide evidence of Servetus' heresy for the Geneva council to consider, and that he also loaned Servetus books for use in preparing his defense. Following Servetus' conviction on the heresy charge, Calvin appealed for a more merciful sentence—beheading instead of burning. His request was refused. Michael Servetus was executed by fire on October 27, 1553. He was the only person executed for heresy in Geneva during Calvin's lifetime.

not yet incarnate as a man, Christ approached mankind as an intermediary between God and man even in the Old Testament. Because of His visible form during these encounters, He was described by those who saw Him as an "angel." Yet, through it all, He retained the glory belonging to God alone.

This same concept was carried on by Hosea. The prophet alluded to the story of Jacob wrestling with the angel, and then he added, "That is the LORD of hosts. The LORD is His memorable name."[1]

Servetus makes absurd claims indeed! Consider that Jacob even declared, "I have seen God face to face."[2] Furthermore, we have the testimony of Paul that it was Christ who led the Israelites in the wilderness.[3] Even though the time of His incarnation was not yet arrived, the eternal Word already was revealing Himself and providing a foreshadowing of the role that He would take on as our Mediator.

An objective reading of the second chapter of Zechariah will show that the Angel who sends other angels is instantly proclaimed to be God Almighty. This is only another of a whole host of Scripture passages which all agree (not that this will convince unbelievers). I will skip over most of these, but I will mention two more. Isaiah says, "Behold, this is our God; we have waited for Him, and He will save us. This is the LORD; we have waited for Him; we will be glad and rejoice in His salvation."[4] Even the blind could see that this passage is referring to God rising up in a new way to save His people.

If Isaiah is not plain enough, Malachi is even more obvious: "'Behold, I send My messenger, and he will prepare the way before Me. And the Lord, whom you seek, will suddenly come to His temple, even the Messenger of the covenant, in whom you delight. Behold, He is coming,' says the LORD of hosts."[5] The temple is consecrated to God alone, and yet Malachi here claims it for the Messiah. Clearly, the Messiah is indeed the same God whom the Israelites had always worshiped.

The Deity of Christ in the New Testament

While there are many proofs of Christ's divinity in the Old Testament, there are even more in the New Testament—so many, in fact, that we cannot possibly cover all of them. Instead, we will look at a brief selection of Bible passages which together conclusively testify to the deity of Christ and His eternal nature.

First, let us consider the teaching of the apostles. They explain again and again that the Old Testament prophecies have been fulfilled in Christ. For example, Isaiah prophesied, "The LORD of hosts, Him you shall hallow; let Him be your fear,

---

[1] Hosea 12:5
[2] Genesis 32:30
[3] I Corinthians 10:4
[4] Isaiah 25:9
[5] Malachi 3:1

and let Him be your dread. He will be as a sanctuary, but a stone of stumbling and a rock of offense to both the houses of Israel, as a trap and a snare to the inhabitants of Jerusalem." Paul declares that Christ was the fulfillment of this prophecy.[1] We can only conclude that Paul was proclaiming Christ to be the LORD Almighty.

Similarly, Paul references Psalm 68 in his letter to the Ephesians: "He ascended on high, He took many captives." The apostle applies the prophecy to Christ, and the Psalm makes it abundantly clear that the verse is speaking about God.[2] We must conclude that Jesus Christ is God.

John testifies that Isaiah saw the glory of Jesus in his vision, although the prophet himself says that he saw the glory of God.[3] Again, we see the deity of Christ proclaimed.

The author of Hebrews ascribes unto Christ the most glorious attributes of God found in the Psalms: "You, LORD, in the beginning laid the foundation of the earth, and the heavens are the work of Your hands." He says also, "Let all the angels of God worship Him."[4] In fact, Christ is set forth as the fulfillment of all prophecies of the Psalms. It is Christ who rises up to have compassion on Zion, and it is Christ who rules the earth and the distant shores.

John certainly would have no hesitation about speaking of the majesty of God in Christ Jesus, having already said that Word was eternally God.[5] Paul did not shrink from placing Christ on the judgment seat of God, having already declared that Jesus Christ is God appearing in flesh, God over all and forever praised.[6] Indeed, Paul was not in the least subtle about his declaration of Christ's deity. He describes Jesus in this way: "who, being in the form of God, did not consider it robbery to be equal with God."[7]

The apostles readily affirm that Jesus Christ is God manifest in the flesh, that God purchased the Church with His own blood. When Thomas said to Jesus, "My Lord and my God," he was proclaiming Christ as the only God, the God whom he had always worshiped.[8]

---

[1] Isaiah 8:13-14, Romans 9:33

[2] Psalm 68:18, Ephesians 4:8

[3] John 12:41, Isaiah 6:4

[4] Hebrews 1:10,6

[5] John 1:1, 14

[6] II Corinthians 5:10, I Timothy 3:16, Romans 9:5

[7] Philippians 2:6

[8] John 20:28

The testimonies of the apostles are compelling proof, but when we consider the works of Christ, we see His divinity even more clearly. When Jesus told the Jews that He had been at work from the beginning with the Father, they immediately tried to kill Him. If they understood nothing else from His teaching, they knew that He was claiming divine power. How much more stupid would we be if, despite all this evidence, we could not grasp even that much truth! The author of Hebrews tells us that Christ sustains the world by His word. That is something which could only be accomplished by God.[1] Isaiah tells us that God is the one who blots out transgressions, but Jesus forgave sins and even performed miracles to demonstrate His power to do so.[2] Only God can search the silent thoughts of our hearts, but Jesus was able to do this as well. Taking all this evidence together, we can only conclude that Jesus is God.

Christ's miracles are the final proof of His divine nature. Certainly, miracles were not unique to Christ. The prophets also performed miracles which were every bit as astonishing as those done by Christ. However, we see an obvious difference in purpose between the miracles of the prophets and the miracles of Christ: the prophets were ministers of God who distributed His gifts, but Christ's miracles demonstrated His own power and authority. Occasionally, Jesus would pray to the Father, thus giving glory to the Father, but overall, we see His own power manifested in His works. In fact, not only did Christ perform miracles by His own authority, but He also dispensed miracle-working power to His apostle, enabling them to raise the dead, cure diseases, cast out demons, and so on.[3] These disciples never hesitated to acknowledge that their miracles were accomplished by the power and authority of Jesus: "In the name of Jesus Christ of Nazareth, rise up and walk."[4]

There is no salvation, no righteousness, and no life apart from God. Christ contains all of these within Himself; He is God revealed to us. I will not hear any more of this talk about God pouring life and salvation into Christ. Jesus does not *receive* salvation. Jesus *is* salvation. No one except God is good. Is Jesus good? I cannot even bring myself to say that He is merely good. He *is* goodness. He is the source from which all goodness flows. John tells us that Christ the Word was alive from the very beginning, and that His life is the light of all mankind.[5]

---

[1] Hebrews 1:3
[2] Isaiah 43:25, Matthew 9:6
[3] Matthew 10:8
[4] Acts 3:6
[5] John 1:1-9

With such clear evidence of Christ's divinity, we dare to put our faith and trust in Him. We would never be so blasphemous as to place our faith in a mere creature, but we know that Christ is eternal God.

The Deity of the Holy Spirit

Having established proof of the divinity of Christ, we should examine the Scriptures for evidence of the deity of the Holy Spirit. We do not have to look far; it is apparent from the very first verses in Genesis: "The Spirit of God was hovering over the face of the waters."[1] This creation account indicates that the universe owes its beauty to the Spirit, and further declares that even before the world took form, the Spirit nurtured the shapeless mass. Divinity is further established by Isaiah when he cries out, "The LORD God and His Spirit have sent me."[2] We observe that the Spirit sends the prophets, a role which can only be filled by God.

Both of those examples exhibit the majesty of the Spirit, but the surest proofs of His deity are found when we compare the attributes of the Spirit to the attributes of a creature. We cannot help but see a vast difference from which we must conclude that the Spirit is not a mere creature. The boundless Spirit infuses everything with life, both in heaven and on earth. Considering that the Spirit is infinite, we cannot categorize Him as a created being. When we meditate on His work of creating and sustaining life, we must conclude that the Holy Spirit is God.

It is amazing enough to know that the Spirit gives life to every living creature, but even more wonderful is the realization that the Spirit renews the hearts of wicked men and women. Scripture tells us in many places that the Spirit regenerates by His own power, not by borrowing power from another source. Like those attributes of Christ which can only be divine, this attribute of the Spirit proves His deity. Paul tells us that "the Spirit searches all things, yes, the deep things of God," while also asking, "Who has known the mind of the Lord? Or who has become His counselor?"[3] By the Spirit, we are washed and sanctified, and every good thing comes from Him.

Pay close attention to Paul's declaration: "But one and the same Spirit works all these things, distributing to each one individually as He wills."[4] Here we see that

---

[1] Genesis 1:2

[2] Isaiah 48:16

[3] I Corinthians 2:10, Romans 11:34

[4] I Corinthians 12:11

the Spirit acts on His own authority; He is the Author and Authority in a manner which can only be characteristic of God Himself.

The Bible never shies away from describing the Holy Spirit as God. Paul tells us that we are God's temple because His Spirit dwells within us.[1] This is a very important point. All of God's promises that He will choose us as His temple are fulfilled only because the Spirit indwells us. Augustine points out that if we were commanded to build the Holy Spirit a temple made out of wood and stone, we would accept this as clear proof of the divinity of the Spirit. (God has a temple; creatures do not.) How much more should we recognize His deity when we ourselves *are* the temple of the Holy Spirit![2]

Again and again, the apostles speak quite directly of the Holy Spirit as God. Peter rebuked Ananias for lying to the Holy Spirit, adding that he did not lie to men but to God.[3] The prophets declared that they spoke the words of God, and Jesus and the apostles ascribe those same words to the Holy Spirit. God complained that He was angered by the stubbornness of the people, and Isaiah wrote: "They rebelled and grieved His Holy Spirit."[4]

Finally, if blasphemy against the Holy Spirit may not be forgiven either in this age or in the one to come, even while blasphemy against the Son may be forgiven, then we must acknowledge that if the Son is divine, the Holy Spirit must certainly be divine also.[5] These are only a few of the proofs which set the minds of believers at ease.

Oneness

God revealed Himself most clearly in the coming of Christ, and so we tend to think in terms of the three Persons of God. However, there are many examples in the Bible which emphasize God's Oneness. For example, Paul connected these three things together: God, faith, and baptism.[6] He reasoned that because there is one faith, there is one God; and because there is one baptism, there is one faith. Therefore, our baptism initiates us into the faith and the worship of one God, and we must believe that He into whose name we are baptized is the one true God.

---

[1] I Corinthians 3:16, I Corinthians 6:19

[2] Augustine, *Ad Maximinum*, Ep 66

[3] Acts 5:3

[4] Isaiah 63:10

[5] Mark 3:29

[6] Ephesians 4:5

History Corner

Arianism was a heresy that rose to great prominence in the 4th century. Arians taught that God the Father created Jesus at some point in time, and that Jesus did not share divine essence with God the Father.

The controversy over Arianism became so intense that Emperor Constantine called the Council of Nicaea to resolve the debate. Arian heresy was soundly defeated at the council, but the teachings continued to plague the church for several more centuries, especially among the Germanic tribes, since they had been evangelized by Arian missionaries.

The **Macedonians** were a heretical sect with many similarities to the Arians. They taught that the Holy Spirit was not eternal, but was created by the Father and the Son.

It is obvious that when Jesus commanded us to "go therefore and make disciples of all the nations, baptizing them in the name of the Father, and of the Son, and of the Holy Spirit,"[1] this is identical to baptism into the name of the one God. It is clear that there are three Persons in God's essence, but there is only one God.

Faith should never be glancing here and there or running this way and that; it should be fixed on one God alone. If there are many kinds of faith, there must be many gods. Our baptism assures us of the unity of God, because there is only one baptism. We are permitted only to be baptized into the name of one God. When Jesus commanded baptism in the name of the Father, and of the Son, and of the Holy Spirit, He can only have meant that we should believe with one faith in the Father, the Son, and the Holy Spirit, who are one God.

Since there is only one God, we must conclude that the Word and the Spirit are the essence of God. Nothing could be sillier than the talk of the Arians who acknowledge the divinity of Christ while denying that He is of divine essence. The Macedonians bluster in an even more ridiculous manner when they claim that "Spirit" refers merely to God's gifts. What foolishness! We know that the Spirit is the source of wisdom, understanding, power, and righteousness, and furthermore, He is the *one* Spirit of wisdom, understanding, power, and righteousness. He is not divided into this gift or that gift. Paul declares that however the gifts are divided, the Holy Spirit remains one and the same.[2]

Threeness

While Scripture demonstrates the Oneness of God, it also reveals a distinction between the Father and the Son, and between the Son and the Holy Spirit. This is a great mystery, and we must be reverent in our discussion of it.

---

[1] Matthew 28:19
[2] I Corinthians 12:11

I deeply admire the words of Gregory of Nazianzus: "No sooner do I conceive of the One than I am illumined by the splendor of the Three; no sooner do I distinguish Them than I am carried back to the One."[1] We should not imagine the Trinity in a way in which the Threeness distracts us too much. We must immediately bring our minds back to the unity of God. The words "Father," "Son," and "Holy Spirit" indicate real distinctions, but distinctions only. These are not *divisions* of God.

The Bible verses quoted in this chapter have already established that the Son is in some manner distinct from the Father. The Word could not have been *with* God unless He had a subsistence which was distinct from the Father. Jesus also indicated this distinction when He said that there is another who bears witness of Him.[2] Furthermore, it was not the Father who came down to earth and became man, but rather Christ who came from the Father. It was not the Father who died and rose from the dead, but it was the Son whom the Father had sent. This distinction between Father and Son did not begin at the incarnation. John tells us that the Son was in the closest relationship with the Father before He was made known.[3] He was with the Father and had His own glory with the Father long before He was revealed in the incarnation.

Jesus implies the distinction between the Holy Spirit and the Father when He says that the Spirit proceeds from the Father.[4] He likewise indicates this distinction between the Holy Spirit and Himself when He declares that He will send a Comforter to us.

> **"I'll take 'Obscure Church Fathers' for $800, Alex!"**
>
> **Gregory of Nazianzus** (c. 325 – 389 AD) is best known for his defense of the Trinity against the heresy of the Arians.
>
> Gregory preferred a simple monastic life, but (through the influence of his father and others) eventually found himself deeply involved in church leadership. His eloquent preaching attracted a large following, and he was appointed Bishop of Constantinople.
>
> Gregory wrote prolifically, especially concerning the Trinity and the relationship between the Persons. In response to the heresies of his day, he declared the eternal deity of Christ.

---

[1] Gregory of Nazianzus, *Nicene and Post-Nicene Fathers, Series II, Vol. 7*, Oration on Holy Baptism, trans. Philip Schaff and Henry Wace, T&T Clark, Edinburgh.

[2] John 5:32

[3] John 1:18

[4] John 15:26

Differences Between the Father, the Son, and the Holy Spirit

I am not certain whether it is completely appropriate to make analogies about the Trinity based on human relationships. The ancient church fathers sometimes did that, but they would also acknowledge the severe limitations of these analogies. I must admit that I am afraid of saying something here which will confuse someone. However, I cannot keep silent about a topic which is clearly found in Scripture, and so I will do my best to explain.

The Bible teaches that differences exist between the Father, the Son, and the Holy Spirit. The Father is referred to as the beginning and source of everything. Wisdom, good counsel, and orderliness are attributed to the Son. Power and effective action are the office of the Holy Spirit. Although all three Persons are eternal (for God could never be without His wisdom and power), there is a sort of arrangement to them. The Father is said to be first, and then the Son coming from the Father, and finally, the Holy Spirit proceeding from the Father and the Son together. The human mind tends to think in that order: (1) God, (2) the wisdom coming from God, (3) the power by which God carries out His plan. This is the reason that the Son is only said to proceed from the Father, while the Spirit proceeds from both the Father and the Son. The progression is evident in many Bible passages, especially Romans 8, in which Paul refers to the Holy Spirit as both the Spirit of Christ and the Spirit of Him who raised up Christ from the dead. Peter also says that it was the Spirit of Christ who spoke through the prophets, even though elsewhere Scripture teaches that it was the Spirit of God the Father.

These differences never interfere with the perfect unity of God. The Son is one with the Father, for they share one Spirit. The Spirit is not divided from the Father and the Son, for He is the Spirit of the Father and the Son. Christ Himself declared that He was in the Father and the Father in Him.[1] Church theologians have always rejected the idea that the Persons of the Trinity are different in essence. Augustine says, "The names which denote distinctions refer to Their relationship one to another, not to the substance by which They are one."[2] Unless we understand this perspective, it may seem to us that the church fathers disagreed on this matter. Some teach that the Father is the beginning of the Son, while others declare that the Son has divinity and essence from Himself and so was with the Father from the beginning. This apparent discrepancy is clearly explained by Augustine: "With

---

[1] John 14:10

[2] Augustine, *On the Trinity*, Book V, Chapter V.

Trinity and the Knowledge of God

Calvin declares that the doctrine of the Trinity is extremely important to a proper understanding of God. Human pride endeavors to reduce God to something more understandable to human minds, but this is unacceptable. Any deviation from a biblical perspective on the Trinity quickly deteriorates into abominable heresy and blasphemy.

The Arians, Macedonians, and others who held non-Trinitarian views ultimately denied the deity of Christ or the Holy Spirit. Without acknowledgement of the deity of the Persons, Christianity crumbles entirely. How can salvation be accomplished by a mere man? Unless Christ is God, our hope is in vain.

Non-Trinitarian sects still exist today, although not as commonly as in the second century. The United Pentecostal Church International (which boasts more than 4,000 churches in the United States and Canada) teaches that Jesus did not exist prior to the incarnation, and that Father, Son, and Holy Spirit are mere titles of God rather than Persons of the Trinity.

---

respect to Himself, Christ is called God. With respect to the Father, He is called Son. With respect to Himself, the Father is called God. With respect to the Son, He is called Father. The One who is called Father (with respect to the Son) is not the Son. The One who is called Son (with respect to the Father) is not the Father."[1] And so, when we speak simply of the Son, we may truthfully say that He is the only beginning. Yet, in the next breath, when we discuss the Son's relationship with the Father, we may say truthfully that the Father has begotten the Son.

The Triune God

I will now summarize the aspects of the Trinity which are important to a proper understanding of the Christian faith: when we say that we believe in one God, we understand this to mean *one essence comprised of three Persons*; and so, whenever we use the name of God, we mean the Father, Son, and Holy Spirit. However, when we compare the Father, Son, and Holy Spirit, we must consider the relationship between them, and so we consider the distinctions between the Persons. These distinctions have a particular order in which the Father is the beginning and source. Therefore, whenever mention is made of the Father and Son together, or of the Father and Spirit together, the name of God is especially bestowed upon the Father. In this way, we describe both the unity of God's essence and the order – an order which in no way diminishes the divinity of the Son and Holy Spirit.

---

[1] Augustine, *On the Trinity*, Book V, Chapter V.

The apostles testified that the Son of God is the same Jehovah spoken of by the prophets. We declare that it is blasphemy to say that Christ is a different God from the Father.

We also acknowledge that the Spirit is called "God" by Christ Himself. Just as the Father and Son are each fully God, the Spirit is also the entire spiritual essence of God – the Father, the Son, and Holy Spirit. The Holy Spirit is God and also from God.

CHAPTER 14
ANGELS AND DEMONS

Searching the Scripture

Since angels are messengers chosen by God to carry out His commands, it is obvious that they are also His creatures. This much we can say with confidence, but there are many things we do not know about them, and it is foolish to speculate too much. For example, arguments about when angels were created or in what order they were created are pointless discussions. The creation account indicates that the earth was completed and the heavens and everything in them were finished. Why bother to agonize about whether angels were created on the same day in which the stars and planets were formed or whether they belong to some distant creation outside this realm?

We will confine our investigation of angels to those things which the Scripture lays out plainly. As always, we should concern ourselves with things which are provided for our edification.

I know that many people have seized

Ol' What's-His-Name

Calvin mentions a book called *Celestial Hierarchy* by Dionysus, adding the dubious qualifier: "whoever he was." Scholars today still refer to him in much the same manner.

Celestial Hierarchy was one of several books penned by a man who referred to himself as "Dionysus." He was generally assumed to be the disciple converted by Paul in Acts 17:34. However, disputes about his real identity stretch all the way back to the 6th century, shortly after the writings mysteriously appeared. Generally, it is now accepted that "Dionysus" (whoever he was) lived in the early 6th century, but no one can positively identify him. Modern scholars have dubbed him "Pseudo-Dionysius."

The writings attributed to Dionysius are heavily mystical. *Celestial Hierarchy* describes the supposed rank and order of angels.

upon the subject of angels in an unhealthy manner. Certainly Dionysus (whoever he was) wrote beautifully about the heavenly realm in his book *Celestial Hierarchy*. However, when you consider his writings, you must admit that they are packed with fantasy. He wrote as if he had been to heaven and had seen these things with his own eyes, and yet the apostle Paul, when he was caught up to the third heaven, declared that he was not permitted to speak about the secret things which he had seen.

The work of a true theologian is not to amuse people, but rather to teach things which are true and beneficial. Keeping this in mind, we will proceed to the simple teaching of Scripture, so that we may learn what God would have us know about angels.

The Role of Angels in Scripture

The main term for angels in the original text of Scripture indicates their role as messengers of God. Other words for them are used as well. They are sometimes referred to as the "heavenly host" because they encircle God like bodyguards surround a prince, proclaiming His grandeur. They are like soldiers carrying the flag of their commander, ready to obey orders. The prophet Daniel recounts his vision of God ascending to the judgment seat: "A thousand thousands ministered to Him; ten thousand times ten thousand stood before Him."[1] Since God works His authority through the angels, they are also sometimes referred to as "powers," "principalities," or "dominions."[2] They are even described several times in Scripture as "gods," doubtless because they reflect God's glory to us.[3] This should not be confused with the Angel of the Lord (Christ) who appeared several times to the patriarchs. I am speaking now of a reference to multiple angels together, when occasionally the word "gods" is used to identify them. This should not surprise us. The Bible even uses the word "gods" to describe earthly princes at times,[4] and why should it not be used to describe the angels? They radiate the glory of God.

The Bible particularly emphasizes the role of the angels as our protectors and helpers. Undoubtedly, this is meant to reassure and comfort believers. Scripture reminds us that angels watch over us, defend us, guide us, and protect us: "For He shall give His angels charge over you, to keep you in all your ways. In their hands they shall bear you up, lest you dash your foot against a stone," and, "The angel of the LORD encamps all around those who fear Him, and delivers them."[5] God commissions the angels to shield those whom He is guarding.

---

[1] Daniel 7:10

[2] Colossians 1:16, Ephesians 1:21, I Corinthians 15:24

[3] Psalm 138:1

[4] Psalm 82:6

[5] Psalm 91:11-12, Psalm 34:7

Let us review a few of the scriptural examples in which angels came to the aid of believers. We are told in Genesis that the angel of the Lord comforted Hagar in the wilderness and instructed her to return to Sarah.[1]   Moreover, God promised Abraham that an angel would guide him on the journey.[2]   When Jacob blessed Ephraim and Manasseh, he prayed that the angel of the Lord who had delivered him from evil would bless them.[3] Whenever God would rescue Israel from the hands of their enemies, He would employ angels to carry the message or even to fight for His people.[4] Angels ministered to Christ in His suffering.[5]   Angels announced the resurrection of Christ to the women who came to the tomb, and they proclaimed at the ascension that He would return in glory.[6] Angels protect us, fighting against Satan and all other enemies of God.

Do We Each Have a Guardian Angel?

I have no confidence whatsoever in the teaching which holds that individual angels are assigned to care for individual believers. It is true that the prophet Daniel mentions the angel of the Persians and the angel of the Greeks,[7] but this reveals nothing more than that specific angels have been appointed over particular kingdoms. Jesus declared that children's angels always behold the face of the Father.[8] This verse does confirm that certain angels are appointed to guard children, but I cannot conclude that each individual child has his own angel.

I believe it would be more accurate to say that all angels together watch over us. Consider that Christ has said that the angels

---

Angel On My Shoulder

Folklore regarding angels is rampant. Sometimes, angels are depicted as adorable children with wings, or as beautiful women singing in choirs. Struggles of conscience are frequently symbolized by an angel and a demon sitting on the shoulders of the afflicted individual. Most common of all is the belief that a particular angel is assigned to each of us as a guardian. Some people even attempt to communicate with "their angel."

Calvin sidesteps many of the pitfalls of discussion about angels. He refuses to guess about the nature of angels. He insists that the reader must remember that the only characteristics of angels we may know with any certainty are those found in Scripture.   All else is speculation and fantasy.

---

[1] Genesis 16:9

[2] Genesis 24:7

[3] Genesis 48:16

[4] Exodus 14:19, Exodus 23:20, Judges 2:1, II Kings 19:35

[5] Matthew 4:11, Luke 22:43

[6] Matthew 28:5-7, Luke 24:5, Acts 1:10

[7] Daniel 10:13, 20

[8] Matthew 18:10

rejoice over the repentance of a sinner.[1] Furthermore, the Bible speaks of multiple angels together bearing Lazarus' soul to Abraham's bosom.[2] Elisha did not show merely one angel to his servant; he revealed a whole host of angels assigned to protect them both.[3]

The only example in Scripture which could possibly be used to support the existence of guardian angels is found in the book of Acts. After Peter escaped from prison, he knocked at the gate of the house where the disciples were staying. Those inside (not believing it was Peter) declared that it must be *his angel*.[4] However, this is unspecific. They could have meant any one of a host of angels rather than a specific angel.

Folklore imagines that we have not merely one angel, but two – a good angel and a bad angel. It is not worthwhile to make a serious investigation of such nonsense. All that I can say is that if someone cannot be content with being under the care of the whole heavenly host, then I do not know how such a person would be comforted at the thought of only one good angel watching over him. It is practically an insult to individual believers and to the larger church when we restrict our care to one angel per person. We should be encouraged that a multitude of the heavenly host surrounds us for our help and protection.

Who Are the Angels?

We will now consider the claims of those who pretend to have knowledge about the number and rank of the angels. We will see whether their teachings are founded upon scriptural truth. It is true that Michael is called "the great prince" by the prophet Daniel, and he is referred to as an archangel in the book of Jude.[5] However, there is no way to extrapolate from these two verses any real sense of the organizational structure of the heavenly host. There are only two names of angels mentioned in Scripture: Michael and Gabriel. Some may also claim Raphael, if they accept the book of Tobit. It could be argued that names are only given to these angels so that we can better grasp their nature and purpose, but I cannot even say that with any certainty.

---

[1] Luke 15:7
[2] Luke 16:22
[3] II Kings 6:17
[4] Acts 12:15
[5] Daniel 12:1, Jude 1:9

Names of Angels

Calvin notes that the Bible identifies two angels by name: Michael and Gabriel. The apocryphal book of Tobit refers to another angel called Raphael. However, Calvin questions whether the names are proper and particular to the angels or whether these "names" are simply titles assumed to explain their role to simple-minded humankind.

The name Michael (meaning "who is like God?") could be a reference to Michael's station as an archangel victorious in battle over the forces of Satan. The name Gabriel ("God is my strength") may reflect his role as a messenger on the authority of God. In the book of Tobit (which Calvin tentatively mentions), the angel Raphael assists a woman afflicted by a demon and helps a man recover his sight. Appropriately, the name of the angel means "God is my healer."

It is noteworthy that the names of angels often appear in a particular context of explanation of their role. For example, the angel who appeared to Zacharias in the first chapter of Luke did not begin by introducing himself. Only when Zacharias doubted his message did the angel declare, "I am Gabriel, who stands in the presence of God."[1]

However, Calvin raises the question of angelic names not to open a new realm of speculation, but rather to make the more general point that there is much we do not know about angels. Even the claim that we know the names of several angels assumes that angels are similar to us in their taking of names. Perhaps angels have proper names as humans do, or perhaps these names are merely assumed for our benefit. We cannot even know this for sure.

Concerning the number of the angels, we know only that there are a multitude of them. Christ referred to them as "legions," while the prophet Daniel spoke of thousands upon thousands.[2] The angels of the Lord are also said to camp around those who fear God,[3] which implies a great number of angels.

As spirits, angels must not have bodies. In order that we may better understand them, however, the Bible describes them as winged creatures called cherubim and seraphim. We should not take this literally; it is meant as a symbol of swiftness. Angels move between heaven and earth like lightning, always arriving in time to bring help.

This summarizes all we know about the order and number of angels. Everything else is a mystery which no mortal will solve in this life. Since this is all that God has chosen to reveal, we should not seek to know more than this or speak as if we know more than we really do.

---

[1] Luke 1:19

[2] Matthew 26:53, Daniel 7:10

[3] Psalm 34:7

Worship of Angels Forbidden

We must now address some of the superstition surrounding angels. People are often inclined to focus too much attention on angels, as though the angels are responsible for the blessings in our lives. As soon as someone attributes blessing to angels directly, it is a short distance from there to worshiping them. In some ages of the church, the glory of God was not declared as it should have been, while angels received great honor.

This is an old problem. Even the apostle Paul had to contend with those who esteemed angels above Christ Himself. Thus he urged the Colossians to remember that the glory of Christ is far above the glory of angels, and that God is the One who blesses us with all good things.[1] We must keep in mind that angels are mere creatures. Any glory angels possess is glory which they receive from God. The splendor of God's majesty shines in them, and it is easy for us to fall down in adoration. Even the apostle John confessed in the book of Revelation that he fell at the feet of an angel, but he also recorded the reaction of the angel: "See that you do not do that! I am your fellow servant, and of your brethren who have the testimony of Jesus. Worship God!"[2]

One way to avoid this danger might be to consider why God employs angels at all. Certainly God does not need them to achieve His purposes. It is not as though God lacks the strength or knowledge to act on His own. God does not turn to the angels for assistance with the difficult task of ruling the universe. In fact, God sometimes completely bypasses the angels and acts directly to declare His glory or protect His children.

Since God does not need angels, the only reasonable conclusion is that He sends them for our sake. We should not need them either. It should be sufficient for us to know that God protects us. But when we find ourselves in the middle of great danger, when trials overwhelm us, and when enemies surround us, we tend to slide into despair. We are silly, frail creatures. God is merciful, and so He sends us comfort better suited to our understanding. He tells us that, in addition to His own constant vigilance for our protection, He has a host of guardians dedicated to our care. With this consolation, we feel greater assurance that God is watching over us, even when danger lurks around us.

---

[1] Colossians 1:16
[2] Revelation 19:10

This extra assurance should be unnecessary. It is a little embarrassing that we cannot be content with the knowledge that our heavenly Father provides for us. The Lord is kind and gentle toward us even in our weakness. We see an example in the account of Elisha's servant in II Kings. The servant saw the mountains overrun by the Syrian army on every side. Realizing that he and prophet were surrounded by enemies, his courage failed. He was overwhelmed with fear, and he cried out to Elisha. Elisha prayed that God would open his servant's eyes. Immediately, the servant glimpsed a host of angels sent for their protection. Encouraged, he recovered his strength. He faced the enemies unafraid.

Let us always remember the reason that God speaks to us of angels, and let us be guided by that principle in our attitude toward them. Our faith in God should be strengthened. We should accept His kindness toward us and be encouraged all the more to trust Him. We should know as Elisha did that "those who are with us are more than those who are with them."[1] Instead of being distracted from the worship of God, we ought to draw closer to Him as we understand this generous provision for our weakness.

We must remember that angels are the instruments of God's work. They do nothing without the direction of God. God is the source of all blessing. Let us never forget the lesson of Jacob's vision. He saw angels descend to earth (to mankind) and ascend again (to God) by a ladder on which the Lord Himself stood.[2] We understand from this symbolism that Christ is the Mediator between God and man. It is through His intercession that angels come to minister to us. Jesus gave the same picture of His work when He said, "Most assuredly, I say to you, hereafter you shall see heaven open, and the angels of God ascending and descending upon the Son of Man."[3]

God did not create angels to share His glory. His intention was never that we should trust them more than we trust Him. Let us bid goodbye to that Platonic philosophy which teaches us to seek God through angels. Angels may seem more

> **Plato's Divine Spirits**
>
> Calvin mentions a "Platonic philosophy" regarding angels. This is a reference to *Epinomis*, a dialogue in Platonic style. Although it has traditionally been included among Plato's works, it is suspected of having been authored by one of Plato's students.
>
> *Epinomis* theorizes that there are divine spirits existing on a level between mortality and immortality. These spirits act as intermediaries between mankind and the gods. *Epinomis* teaches that it is proper to offer prayers to the divine spirits.

---

[1] II Kings 6:16
[2] Genesis 28:12-13
[3] John 1:51

familiar, more like us, and therefore more approachable. Superstition always feels more comfortable (which is why this worship of angels has been so prevalent from the very beginning), but it twists and distorts true Christianity.

Demons

Everything the Bible tells us about demons warns us to be wary of their deceit and to arm ourselves with weapons against them. The Bible calls Satan the god and prince of this world. Peter pictures Satan as a "roaring lion," and then adds in the next verse: "Resist him, steadfast in the faith, knowing that the same sufferings are experienced by your brotherhood in the world."[1] Paul advises us: "For we do not wrestle against flesh and blood, but against principalities, against powers, against the rulers of the darkness of this age, against spiritual hosts of wickedness in the heavenly places. Therefore take up the whole armor of God, that you may be able to withstand in the evil day, and having done all, to stand."[2]

We have been put on guard. We know that our enemy is bold, crafty, and well-armed. We must not allow ourselves to be careless or cowardly. Let us stand with all courage of faith in the battle, calling out to God for help and trusting in His strength alone. Wisdom, strength, courage, and weapons for the battle are all supplied by our Lord.

Scripture warns us that we war against not merely one or two enemies, but against great armies of evil. Mary Magdalene was possessed by seven demons, and Christ explained that a demon once cast out could return with seven others more wicked than himself.[3] A whole legion of evil spirits tormented one man.[4] These examples are provided so that we may understand the seriousness of our circumstances. It is crucial that we realize that we stand against a vast multitude of enemies; we must never become lazy in our warfare.

The Bible often mentions Satan (also calling him the devil), emphasizing that there is a kingdom of evil. Just as Christ is the Head of the church, the forces of darkness have their own leader who rules over them. Thus Jesus declares to the wicked, "Depart from Me, you cursed, into the everlasting fire prepared for the devil and his angels."[1]

---

[1] I Peter 5:8-9

[2] Ephesians 6:12-13

[3] Mark 16:9, Luke 11:26

[4] Mark 5:9

[5] Matthew 25:41

Satan's Delusion

Theologians often differentiate between the **revealed will** of God and the **decretal will** of God. God's commands are His **revealed will**. People can either obey the command or disobey the command. God's eternal plan is His **decretal will**. God sovereignly predestines all things which occur, both good and bad. No one can resist God's decretal will.

Calvin will discuss this idea in much more detail in Chapter 16, but he introduces the first arguments in this chapter. The Bible tells us that Satan rebels against God. Yet Satan also serves God's purposes. Despite his bitterness against God's authority, Satan ultimately fulfills God's plan, even amid his rebellion.

In other words, Satan refuses to obey God's revealed will, while at the same time conforming to God's decretal will. *Every* creature conforms to God's decretal will, even those who refuse to obey His revealed will.

The irony is that Satan hates God and would never willingly obey Him, and yet Satan serves the purposes of God.

The Battle

Scripture refers to Satan as God's enemy and our enemy. This fact alone should stir believers to battle against him. If we have zeal for the glory of God, then we must wage war against evil forces in rebellion against Him. If we acknowledge the lordship of Christ, then we must fight the enemies who seek to destroy His kingdom. If we even care about our own salvation, we can never make peace with one who constantly tries to ensnare us.

Satan plots both the destruction of God's kingdom and the ruin of mankind. In the Garden of Eden, he set out to harm both at once. He convinced Adam and Eve to disobey God (robbing Him of the honor due Him), and he simultaneously flung all humanity into sin and misery.[1] The gospel of Matthew calls Satan our enemy and accuses him of planting weeds in order to corrupt the harvest.[2] In all Satan's works, we find the same obsession with the destruction of God's kingdom. Christ declared that Satan "was a murderer from the beginning, and does not stand in the truth, because there is no truth in him."[3]

In spite of all of this, we must remember that Satan cannot do anything outside the will of God. We read in Job that Satan presented himself before the

---

[1] Genesis 3
[2] Matthew 13:25
[3] John 8:44

Lord to request permission of Him.[1] We learn also that Satan was the instrument of God to bring about the downfall of Ahab; Satan became a lying spirit among the prophets.[2] The evil spirit tormenting Saul punished him for his rebellion against God, and the plagues of Egypt were even said to be the work of "angels of destruction" unleashed by God.[3] Paul declares that God is the one who sends strong delusion on unbelievers, even though in other verses, he calls it a work of Satan.[4]

Satan is obviously under the power of God. Whatever his intentions might be, he still serves God's purpose. We may truthfully say that Satan opposes God, and yet this opposing can go no further than God allows it. I am speaking only of the practical effect of Satan's efforts. He does not serve God by choice; he rebels against God at every turn. His wickedness compels him to seek out new and better ways to war against God. However, he is restrained by God and only able to carry out those things which God allows. Therefore, whether he likes it or not, Satan serves the Lord.

Victory

Evil spirits may fight against believers, disturb and weary them, even terrify and injure them. However, the forces of evil can never completely crush a believer. God limits their activity so that they cannot destroy His people. The wicked are ensnared and defeated; demons take possession of their minds and bodies and enslave them for all manner of shameful purposes.

Believers are not destroyed by Satan and his armies in the same manner or to the same extent in which unbelievers are crushed by them, but Christians should still heed the warning to give no place to the devil.[5] Peter warned us to resist Satan and stand firm in the faith.[6] Paul confessed that he was not above these struggles: "And lest I should be exalted above measure by the abundance of the revelations, a thorn in the flesh was given to me, a messenger of Satan to buffet me, lest I be exalted above measure."[7]

---

[1] Job 1:6
[2] I Kings 22:20-22
[3] I Samuel 16:14, Psalm 78:49
[4] II Thessalonians 2:9, Ephesians 2:2
[5] Ephesians 4:27
[6] I Peter 5:8-9
[7] II Corinthians 12:7

This sort of battle is common to all God's children. Since we have the promise that Christ crushed Satan's head, we know that we can never be conquered by Satan. We may be wounded in the battle. We may fall under terrible blows, but afterward, God raises us up. The injuries are not fatal. In the end, we will be victorious.

I am not saying that every believer will succeed in absolutely everything. Even the elect are vulnerable to Satan's deceptions and may be ensnared by him from time to time. We know that God's work of justice resulted in David being handed over to Satan for a time.[1] Paul acknowledges that some people are caught in Satan's snare who might someday escape from the grasp of the devil and repent.[2] Paul also reveals that the promise that Christ will crush the head of Satan has its fulfillment over time, as we struggle against the forces of evil each day: "And the God of peace will crush Satan under your feet shortly. The grace of our Lord Jesus Christ be with you. Amen."[3]

In Christ our Head, this victory has always been ours, because He is our Lord, and Satan has nothing in Him. We are the body of Christ. As we put off the body of the sins of the flesh and are filled with the Spirit of God, the victory over Satan is complete.

As Christ's kingdom rises, Satan falls. Jesus sent His disciples out to preach the good news of the kingdom, and when they returned, He said, "I saw Satan fall like lightning from heaven."[4] He added later, "When a strong man, fully armed, guards his own palace, his goods are in peace. But when a stronger than he comes upon him and overcomes him, he takes from him all his armor in which he trusted, and divides his spoils."[5] When Christ died, He defeated Satan and all his forces; He conquered death.

Satan is still defeated. Yet Christ must protect His church every day or else Satan would destroy it in an instant. Without the help of God, how could we hold out even for a moment against such power and fury? God's strength sustains us. God does not permit Satan to rule over the souls of the elect. Only those who are not among God's children can be dragged away by the forces of the enemy. Paul says that the god of this age (Satan) has blinded those who do not believe and

---

[1] II Samuel 24:1
[2] II Timothy 2:25-26
[3] Romans 16:20
[4] Luke 10:18
[5] Luke 11:21-22

the devil carries out his work in the sons of disobedience.[1] Yet this is all according to the proper justice of God. The wicked have deteriorated into the image of Satan, and they can only be recognized as the children of the devil. The children of God are renewed in the image of Christ.[2]

---

[1] II Corinthians 4:4, Ephesians 2:2
[2] I John 3:8-10

CHAPTER 15
BODY AND SOUL

The Creation of Mankind

I asserted at the beginning of this book that we must know ourselves in order to fully know God. With this in mind, we turn now to a discussion of mankind. We will investigate the nature of man in its two phases: before the Fall and after the Fall.

Let us begin by considering mankind before the Fall, when our nature was still untouched by sin. As we proceed with this discussion, we must guard against the natural tendency to blame our current sinful inclinations on God. People are always looking for a way to shift the blame for their actions anywhere they possibly can—even to God Himself! Some people who prefer to think of themselves as reverent may never come out and say God is to blame for their imperfections, but they still blame "nature." This is only a more subtle means of insulting God. After all, He is the Creator of nature.

> **Theodicy [thee-oh'-du-see] - noun**
>
> **Theodicy** is the vindication of God's holiness and justice. Calvin has a strong interest in theodicy throughout his work. He places the blame for sin on mankind, while defending God's justice and mercy.

We must be cautious in our approach to this topic so that we may avoid this self-righteous trap. In this chapter, I will show my readers that mankind is completely without excuse. After I have established that God is not to blame for our sinful condition, I will explain how very far we have fallen from that state of perfection in which Adam lived at the beginning.

Although humans are a wonderful creation of God, we should never forget that we were dust before God formed us. It is ridiculous that creatures formed from dirt go around bragging about their supposed superiority. God graciously breathed life into dust which He formed into a man, and He made our bodies to be vessels of immortal spirits. Adam could not boast of his own excellence, yet he could rejoice greatly in the generosity of his Creator.

Soma Sema?

Some theologians have argued that Calvin reveals a heavy Platonic influence in his chapter on the nature of body and soul. Admittedly, Calvin's phrasing does bear a remarkable resemblance to Plato's philosophy called **soma sema** ("the body is the tomb").

In his dialogues, Plato contends that souls exist prior to human birth and that souls who fail to keep their eyes on spiritual light are dragged down and imprisoned in bodies. According to Plato, the soul has served its sentence when the body dies, and it is freed once again.

Calvin does refer to the body as the "prison-house" of the soul, and he says that the spirit is set free at death. However, beyond this similarity in terminology, his theology bears little resemblance to soma sema. Calvin never supports pre-existence of souls, and he often speaks very highly of material creation. His writings reveal no sympathy for Manichaeism or other philosophies which promote the idea that matter is evil.

Most likely, Calvin's comment regarding the body as a "prison-house" refers to the current condition of humankind. We are immortal souls contained within perishing bodies. The apostle Paul declares in Romans 8 that we all groan inwardly as we await the redemption of our bodies. At death, our spirits are freed (under the guardianship of God) to await the resurrection.

Paul wrote to the Philippians: "For our citizenship is in heaven, from which we also eagerly wait for the Savior, the Lord Jesus Christ, who will transform our lowly body that it may be conformed to His glorious body, according to the working by which He is able even to subdue all things to Himself."[1]

Body and Soul

Each person consists of a body and a soul. This should be beyond serious argument. I use the term "soul" to indicate an essence which is created and yet is also immortal. It is the noblest part of a person. Sometimes we may call it a "spirit." When the terms "soul" and "spirit" are used together, they may have different shades of meaning, but when we speak solely about a person's "spirit," it is a simple reference to the person's soul. An example of this terminology can be found in Ecclesiastes, where Solomon speaks of death and says that "the spirit returns to God

---

[1] Philippians 3:20-21

who gave it."[1] Christ committed His spirit to the Father when He died, and Stephen prayed that Jesus would receive his spirit.[2] When the body dies and the soul is set free from its prison-house, God is its guardian.

Some people think that the reference to the soul as a "spirit" indicates that it is transient—a force breathed into us which dissipates at death. What a silly idea! People feel tied to the earth more than they should, and so they do not think they will live on after death. The existence of the human conscience is one proof of our immortality. If

> **Immortality of Souls**
>
> Calvin shakes his head at the absurdity of those who claim that the soul dies with the body. He presents multiple reasons we may be certain that souls are immortal.
>
> Among these is a critical point that humans are made in God's image. We must be created for eternity if we reflect the likeness of God.

we did not have an instinctive knowledge of the judgment facing us after death, why would we be bothered by our sinful actions? Why would we be in terror of God's wrath if death is the end of everything?

The human mind is implanted with all manner of gifts that whisper of something divine, something immortal. Animals do not sense anything beyond their immediate circumstances; they are fixed within their physical bodies. In contrast, the human mind is never content to circle around the body. It stretches out, reaching toward heaven, searching the earth, delving into the secrets of nature. The human mind sets things in order, recognizes patterns, and predicts future events based upon knowledge of the past and the present. Our intelligence enables us to comprehend the idea of an invisible God, which is something that a body could never do. We understand concepts of justice, righteousness, and honor, even though these are not apparent to any of our five bodily senses. We can only conclude that the soul is the force behind this intelligence.

The soul and body cannot be inseparable. If they were, how could the Bible say that we dwell in houses of clay?[3] At death, we leave behind this casing of flesh so that we may receive a reward in heaven. Scripture refers to the separation of body and soul on many occasions. Paul instructs believers to cleanse themselves from all filthiness of flesh and spirit.[4] When he phrases it this way, he distinguishes between

---

[1] Ecclesiastes 12:7

[2] Luke 23:46, Acts 7:59

[3] Job 4:19

[4] II Corinthians 7:1

the two parts of a person which are tainted by the filthiness of sin—our bodies and our souls. Peter referred to Christ as the Shepherd and Overseer of souls. In order for Peter to make this statement, there must be souls for Christ to shepherd. Indeed, if souls did not exist, there would also be little point in discussing the salvation of souls or urging believers to abstain from fleshly lusts which war against our souls.[1] Furthermore, the author of Hebrews states that pastors must watch over the souls of their flocks and render an account, which would be nonsense if there were no souls.[2] The clearest expression may be in Christ's words when He says, "Do not fear those who kill the body but cannot kill the soul. But rather fear Him who is able to destroy both soul and body in hell."[3]

Unless the soul lives on after the death of the body, it would be misleading for Christ to describe the soul of Lazarus safe in Abraham's bosom and the soul of the rich man tormented in fire.[4] Paul teaches the same concept in II Corinthians 5: "So we are always confident, knowing that while we are at home in the body we are absent from the Lord. For we walk by faith, not by sight. We are confident, yes, well pleased rather to be absent from the body and to be present with the Lord."[5]

I feel that I am belaboring a subject which should present no great difficulty to anyone. I could give many more proofs, but I will provide only one last point: the great error of the Sadducees was that they did not believe in spirits or angels.

Mankind Reflects God's Image

Humans are created in the image of God. This is yet another proof of the existence of their immortal souls. Even our bodies differ from those of ordinary animals: "Other living things are bent downward toward the earth, but mankind has been given a face which is raised up to look toward the heavens and to gaze upon the stars."[6] God's glory shines in the design of the human body, and there are whispers of eternity in everything around us, yet there is no doubt that the soul is the clearest reflection of God.

The astounding gift of human intellect reflects the glory of God. This is especially evident when we

---

[1] I Peter 2:25, I Peter 1:9

[2] Hebrews 13:17

[3] Matthew 10:28

[4] Luke 16:22-23

[5] II Corinthians 5:6-8

[6] Ovid, *Metamorphoses*, Book I.

History Corner

Publius Ovidius Naso (43 BC – 17 AD) was a Roman poet known for his erotic and mythological poetry. He is commonly referred to as **Ovid** in literary works today.

Calvin quotes Ovid's famous mythological poem *Metamorphoses*.

consider our restoration in Christ. When Adam fell, he was separated from God. God's image was not completely destroyed in him, but it was twisted and broken. In Christ, we are renewed. Jesus is called the Second Adam because He restores us to the full likeness of God. The apostle Paul contrasts the First Adam and the Second Adam to make the point that there is a greater measure of grace in our renewal than in our original creation. However, his overall point still stands that this renewal re-creates us in the image of God.[1] Paul also urges us: "Put on the new man which was created according to God, in true righteousness and holiness."[2]

Notice that Paul focuses on righteousness and holiness as ways in which we are renewed. God's image is chiefly reflected in illumination of mind and uprightness of character. Paul speaks to the Corinthians about this transformation: "But we all, with unveiled face, beholding as in a mirror the glory of the Lord, are being transformed into the same image from glory to glory, just as by the Spirit of the Lord."[3]

Christ is the perfect image of God. We are changed day by day to be like Him, and so we are restored to true holiness, purity, and wisdom.

The Soul

We should not look to the philosophers for our definition of a "soul." Scarcely even one of them (except possibly Plato) will so much as admit that the soul is immortal. Other philosophers may mention the possibility here and there, but so vaguely that it is obvious they have no idea what they are talking about. Plato does say that the soul reflects the image of God, and so, of all of them, he could be considered the most accurate. Others view the gifts and abilities of the soul as attached so strongly to the present life that they fail to consider the soul's separation from the body.

The Bible teaches us that the soul is a spirit. Under normal circumstances, a spirit is not limited by spatial boundaries, but in our particular situation, it is encased in a body. It lives there like it is in a house, filling the body with life and purpose and, most of all, giving it a desire to know God. We may not always consciously realize the natural human desire for God, and yet we see it in everything people do. Why are people so concerned about what others think of them if not

---

[1] Colossians 3:10

[2] Ephesians 4:24

[3] II Corinthians 3:18

because they know they should be ashamed of themselves? And why would people be ashamed of themselves if not because they admire righteousness? On some level, they are aware that they were created to be good and that they are falling short of their intended purpose. The knowledge of God is deeply imprinted upon the human soul, and no one can be truly happy apart from God. Since the soul is the seat of knowledge, all reason is inextricably bound up with our desire for God. The closer we draw to God, the more we prove ourselves to be reasonable people.

We should reject the notion that more than one soul inhabits each person. The philosophers ramble on about a "sensitive soul" and a "rational soul," and while there is some truth to things that they say, there is much baseless speculation. They claim that there is a great discrepancy between emotion and intellect, and so they conclude that these must be separate entities. They are correct in that there is often a disagreement between our emotion and our intellect, but there is also often a sort of war *within* the intellect as well. This is the natural result of having a fallen nature, and so I do not see why anyone would assume that the disagreement of emotion and intellect would indicate multiple souls.

> **"Whatever."**
>
> Calvin makes some faint effort at dissecting the views of the philosophers about the characteristics of the soul before he waves them all aside as inconsequential speculation. He admits that some things said by the philosophers may be interesting, and he confesses his preference for Plato, but ultimately, he dismisses all of them.
>
> Calvin concludes that all philosophers, however right or wrong they were in their theories in other respects, are missing a key piece of the puzzle: mankind is fallen. No amount of education or self-improvement can fix the fundamental brokenness of the human soul.

Some of the philosophers' teachings are interesting, and some are even true. I would never tell my readers not to learn philosophy. However, I fear that these books have the potential to lead us into useless nitpicking and speculation which is ultimately unhelpful. I am not strongly opposed to classifying personality types or principles of action. The philosophers may divide this aspect of the soul from that aspect, telling us that we are ruled by appetites and understanding, and discussing how understanding motivates the will. They may talk about how good and evil are contemplated by the reason for the purpose of living rightly and so on. However, the philosophers make a critical error: they assume that reason enables a person to live a righteous life. So we are forced away from the teachings of the philosophers because of their ignorance regarding the corruption of human nature.

I propose that there are two aspects of the soul: intellect and will. The intellect judges between various objects or ideas according to whether they should be approved or disapproved. The will chooses to follow the judgment of the intellect. We will not bother with Aristotle and his theory about the appetitive intellect. Let us not be caught up in such trivial nonsense. We will stick to a simple definition of intellect as the guide and ruler of the soul, while the will waits for its decisions in order to proceed with action.

Free Will

God has provided the soul of each person with intellect—the ability to discern good from evil, justice from injustice. Reason is like a lamp whereby we are able to know which things to follow and which to avoid. God has also given to each soul a will. The will makes choices.

Before mankind's rebellion against God, humans excelled in both understanding and choice. Reason, wisdom, and judgment were sufficient not only to properly govern earthly life, but even to enable mankind to rise up to eternal happiness in God. God gave humans the ability to choose according to their understanding.

We would be getting ahead of ourselves to begin a discussion of God's secret predestination at this point. Our topic at the moment is not what could happen in God's eternal plan. We are discussing human nature. From this perspective, we can truly say that Adam sinned by his own choice. He could have chosen obedience to God, but he did not. He lacked perseverance in righteousness. He fell so easily. Yet he had a free choice. In fact, he had what all those after him have lacked: uprightness of mind and will, with a natural predisposition towards obedience to God. He destroyed himself, corrupting all the good gifts which God had given him.

The philosophers grope in the dark because they do not understand this basic corruption of human nature. They are searching around an old ruin, looking for a complete building. They are gathering up scattered pieces and trying to view them as a proper structure. The philosophers claim that humans could not be rational creatures unless they were given free choice between good and evil. They further declare that the difference between good and evil would be meaningless unless humans could plan their own lives. So far, so good. If there had been no corruption of the human nature, this would be perfectly appropriate reasoning. However, since the philosophers lack understanding of the sinful nature, they launch into hopeless confusion.

Professing Christians would be foolish to attempt a serious compromise between philosophers and Christian doctrine. The philosophers hold out hope for man's free will while all mankind is drowning in spiritual destruction. We will discuss this more in future chapters, but for now, let us keep in mind that Adam and Eve before the Fall were far different from all who have come after. We have all inherited a defect from Adam's sin.

Adam was created for righteousness; he was sound in mind. He was free to choose goodness. If anyone complains that God did not make Adam strong enough to resist evil, I can only respond that we cannot pin blame on God. God is not under contract to form humans who lack the ability to sin. I agree that I personally would prefer to be unable to sin. However, the reasons for God's decision are deep within His eternal plan and far beyond our understanding. Let us then simply conclude that Adam was able to choose obedience to God if he had wanted to do so. He lacked perseverance in righteousness. We cannot excuse him; he received from God all the proper gifts to choose right. Adam brought his destruction on himself. Yet God used this for His glory.

Was Calvin a Calvinist?

The debate between Calvinism and Arminianism is often mischaracterized as a dispute between predestination and free will. Many readers are surprised then to read Calvin's defense of the doctrine of free will. Calvin even declares that Adam had the freedom to choose between obedience and disobedience.

Calvin indisputably believed in the reality of free will, and yet he also accepted predestination. Ultimately, he did not preach an either/or approach to the subject; he acknowledged both. He wrote that Adam was free to make a choice, and yet God also predestined Adam's decision for His glory.

Calvinists today also acknowledge that God's decree has established our free choices. Calvinists and Arminians disagree not on the existence of free will, but on the means of salvation. Arminian theologians teach that there is some goodness in the human heart which permits us to choose God. Calvinists argue that humankind is completely incapacitated by sin, and therefore salvation is completely a gift of God and not the result of any goodness within ourselves.

CHAPTER 16
PROVIDENCE

Creation and Providence

God created the world. Most people understand at least this much. Yet there is a tendency for people to acknowledge God as Creator in a distant way, as if He formed the world and everything in it and then stepped back. Those who look upon creation in this manner do not fully understand what the Bible means when it speaks of God creating the world.

The book of Hebrews declares, "By faith we understand that the worlds were framed by the word of God."[1] Why by faith? Surely, it does not take any particular level of faith to look around at the world and realize that it must have a Designer. Even unbelievers may acknowledge that God formed the world and set all things in motion. Their error lies in imagining that the motion is self-sustaining.

Faith requires more of us. By faith, we know that God is the Maker of all things, and we further believe that He still rules over all things. God sustains and cares for everything He has created, even little sparrows.[2]

Scripture is replete with examples of this connection between creation and providence. In Psalm 33, David says that the universe was created by God, and then he continues immediately into a description of God's providence. He begins, "By the word of the LORD the heavens were made, and all the host of them by the breath of His mouth," and then he adds, "The LORD looks from heaven; He sees all the sons of men."[3]

Most people who believe that God is our Creator also believe that He sustains the world in some measure, even if they do not reason it out very clearly. Overall, the philosophers taught (and most people agree) that every corner of the universe is stirred by the presence of God. Yet they did not venture as far as David

---

[1] Hebrews 11:3
[2] Matthew 10:29
[3] Psalm 33:6,13

and the rest of the faithful who declare: "These all wait for You, that You may give them their food in due season. What You give them they gather in; You open Your hand, they are filled with good. You hide Your face, they are troubled; You take away their breath, they die and return to their dust. You send forth Your Spirit, they are created; and You renew the face of the earth."[1]

Pagans may write that we live and move and have our being in God, but they say this without any real awareness of the grace in which we constantly dwell. They do not know God as their Father.

Fate and Chance

Because unbelievers do not understand God's providence, they believe things happen by chance. Suppose a certain man encounters thieves and is robbed, or suppose he is shipwrecked by a storm at sea, or suppose a tree falls on him and kills him. And then perhaps another man wandering through the desert happens to find help, or reaches harbor in spite of the storm, or barely escapes terrible danger. Unbelievers generally say that these things are due to luck—bad luck or good luck.

> **Remember!**
>
> The apostle Paul quoted pagan poet **Epimenides** when he said, "In Him we live and move and have our being."[2]
>
> Calvin alludes to this in order to demonstrate that even pagans have some awareness of God, but they do not really know Him as their heavenly Father.

Christians do not believe in luck. Christ has taught us that even the hairs of our head are counted by God.[3] We know that God rules over everything that happens. God has given us natural laws by which the world operates, and yet none of these laws acts apart from God's decree. Natural events are God's tools by which He carries out His plan in the world. He turns nature this way and that way to accomplish His goals.

The sun is the most amazing thing visible to us. It lights up the whole earth. Its heat warms all living things and enables them to survive. The rays of the sun cause the plants to grow – first warming the seeds underground, then nourishing the little seedlings so that they flourish and bear fruit. Yes, the sun is marvelous! Yet God does not permit us to be so impressed by the sun that we forget that He is the Author and Sustainer of all. To help us remember, He caused light to shine and

---

[1] Psalm 104:27-30

[2] Acts 17:28

[3] Matthew 10:30

plants to appear on the earth before He even created the sun.[1] God demonstrated that He does not need the sun to sustain the earth. He is completely capable of providing light and nourishing plants without the assistance of the sun. Nor should we imagine that the sun (now that it has been created) is beyond the control of God. Scripture tells us that the sun stood still in the sky when Joshua prayed and that the shadow turned back ten degrees as a sign to King Hezekiah.[2] Through these miracles, God testifies that the sun is not rising and setting by some empty habit of nature. He rules over all. He governs the day and night. He decrees the progression of the seasons from winter to spring, and from spring to summer, and from summer to autumn, and back to winter again. All of these so-called "natural events" are administered by the providence of God.

Providence

The Lord proclaims that He is omnipotent. His power is not distant or lazy (although many people imagine it that way). God is watchful and active, always doing. He does not stand far off, casually commanding things to carry on as usual. He directs everything that happens. When we say that He rules over heaven and earth by His providence, we mean that He regulates everything and that nothing occurs except at His command. The psalmist said that God does whatever He pleases.[3] Believers may find comfort in the knowledge that they are always in God's hands.

[1] Genesis 1
[2] Joshua 10:13, II Kings 20:11
[3] Psalm 115:3

Kind Calvinism

Throughout much of this chapter, Calvin argues against a belief system which we would refer to as **deism** today (although the term was unknown in Calvin's era). Deists teach that God created the universe, set certain natural laws to run it, and then left it to follow its own course with no further involvement from Him.

Calvin shivers at the very idea that mankind would be left alone to combat the merciless forces of nature. He exclaims that nature itself proclaims God's sovereign authority.

Calvin extends this argument beyond deism, demonstrating that other philosophies are also attempts to push God away. Yet, if God were further away, this would mean that we had been abandoned.

The doctrine of providence may initially sound harsh, but it is ultimately the only way we can view the universe with any sense of comfort. Life is hard. Even if we do not understand why God sends certain trials to us, we have consolation in knowing that He holds us securely in His hands, and that He will work all things for good.

The alternative is to believe that we are left to the whims of Satan and the blind machinery of nature. Those who insist that bad things happen apart from God's providence are really saying that God has no control over the world and that everything is chance.

Teachers who claim that God works only by setting in motion the laws of nature are insulting the glory of God. Moreover, nothing could be worse for humanity than to be left vulnerable to every motion of the sky, air, earth, and water. God is too kind to abandon us to the whims of nature. David declared that even nursing infants proclaim the glory of God,[1] because (by the merciful design of God) food is provided for them as soon as they emerge from the womb.

People who are aware of God's mighty power achieve a better understanding of life. They realize that God is good and also that He is able to do good things for His children. They trust in His protection, knowing that He is able to defend them against Satan and all other enemies. They are not subject to superstition, because they understand that the power of all creatures is limited by the providence of God.

> **Providence [prov'-i-duhns] - noun**
>
> The word **providence** is derived from the Latin term **providentia**, which indicates foresight, the ability to see ahead. We use the word **providence** to refer to God's benevolent care of His creatures. Calvin points out that God's providence means more than mere knowledge of future events. God does know the future, but He also acts to carry out everything that happens.

Let me clarify that when I speak of God's providence, I am not speaking of mere foreknowledge. God does not sit helplessly in heaven watching events happen on earth. He rules over everything—He sees, and He also acts. When Abraham said to Isaac, "God will provide,"[2] he was not saying merely that God knew what was going to happen. He meant that he could leave the entire matter to God, because God is able to provide a way out of difficult circumstances.

Too many people speak of God's providence as foreknowledge alone. This error is not as extreme as the confusion of those who doubt God's involvement in the universe entirely, but it is still an error which should be challenged. Those teachers who limit providence in such a manner end up claiming that all creatures can move around independently, completely out of God's governance. They say that God moves the hearts of humans by inspiration and persuasion alone.

Far worse are the teachings of the Epicureans (a plague on the earth almost from the beginning) who view God as too lazy to be involved in the events of the world. Other equally ridiculous philosophers claim that God is too far away to see much and has left everything to chance. Even the animals would cry out against such heedlessness!

---

[1] Psalm 8:2
[2] Genesis 22:8

Our Daily Bread

Theologians often differentiate between **general providence** (God's overall supervision of His creation) and **special providence** (particular acts of provision for specific individuals). Calvin accepts that there general rules by which God acts in the world, but he intentionally blurs the distinction between general providence and special providence. He declares that everything God does is purposeful. Each rainstorm arrives because God has willed it; each animal behaving instinctively still acts at the direction of God.

Calvin emphasizes that God is our Father. Our Father may set certain rules, but He does everything with our care in mind. Calvin adds that most Christians realize this on some level, even if they consciously deny it. After all, if God did not act to send rain on the crops and make wheat grow, why would we pray asking our Father in heaven to give us our daily bread? When we pray such things, we acknowledge the special providence within general providence.

General Providence and Special Providence

I intend now to refute that commonly held notion that God directs things in a blind and passive way. This treacherous doctrine confesses that God is the source of all motion the universe, but it does not admit that God purposefully directs events on the earth by His hidden wisdom. According to this teaching, God is the ruler of the universe only in name; all real power is stripped from Him and given to blind forces of nature. After all, there is no sense in saying that God rules over everything unless He actually regulates everything.

I admit that there is a grain of truth amid this error. A sort of general providence exists in which things commonly follow the course of nature. Still, I would carefully qualify that statement by adding that this general providence is not a distant force by which God maintains some pattern in nature, but rather it is the means by which God carefully orders each of His works. It is true that each species within creation is guided by instinct along a particular course which God has set out. This is merely an everyday example of what Christ said: "My Father has been working until now, and I have been working," and also Paul: "In Him we live and move and have our being."[1] The author of Hebrews, proving the divinity of Christ, said that He upholds all things by the word of his power.[2]

While it is true that general providence exists, we must not deny the existence of special providence. Special providence is taught so clearly in Scripture

---

[1] John 5:17, Acts 17:28

[2] Hebrews 1:3

that I am amazed anyone can doubt it. Indeed, those who try to deny it are compelled to modify their doctrines again and again to add exceptions in which God acts with special care for particular creatures. It is a mistake to view these as exceptions at all.

All events occur because God has ordained them; nothing happens by chance. Those who claim that God has set in motion certain repeating patterns of nature emphatically deny that God has anything to do with such things as season changes or weather patterns. They say that events run according to laws of nature, and while sometimes we may have dizzying heat and terrible drought, and other times we may have so much rain that the crops rot, none of these things should be attributed in any way to God. They teach that God has blessed us enough by setting in motion a system in which the earth and sky produce food for us, but that we should not look for the hand of God in more than that.

It would take too much time to list out all the possible arguments against this shabby, heathen view of God. The Word of God should be more than enough for us on this matter. In the Old Testament, God repeatedly declares that the dew and rain are blessings from His hand, and also that crops are destroyed by storms and hail at His command. David sings that God provides food even for young ravens.[1] When God threatens a land with famine, is not this a plain declaration that all creatures are fed by Him? It is childish to try to limit God's involvement in the world to particular acts, when Christ so openly declares that a sparrow does not fall to the ground apart from the will of the Father.[2] If God's will governs even the flight of birds, surely we must acknowledge (as the psalmist proclaims) that God who dwells on high humbles Himself to behold the things that are in the heavens and in the earth.[3]

God Reigns over Mankind

Since we know that the world was established primarily for mankind, we must keep this purpose in mind when we consider how God governs events. The prophet Jeremiah exclaims, "O LORD, I know the way of man is not in himself; it is not in man who walks to direct his own steps."[4] The book of Proverbs says, "A man's steps are of the LORD; how then can a man understand his own way?"[5]

---

[1] Psalm 147:9
[2] Matthew 10:29
[3] Psalm 113:5-6
[4] Jeremiah 10:23
[5] Proverbs 20:24

Considering these Bible passages, can anyone still say that people are free to go any direction they please? If that were so, then each person would be fully able to choose which way to go. Jeremiah and Solomon both make it abundantly clear that they are not even merely speaking of God enabling someone to act, but rather God sovereignly decreeing the outcome. In another proverb, Solomon says, "The preparations of the heart belong to man, but the answer of the tongue is from the LORD."[1] If a man cannot even speak without the direction of God, it would be amazing indeed if he could suddenly start acting without God's governance!

Moreover, Scripture tells us that even events which seem to occur completely by chance are subject to God's decree. Proverbs 16:3 speaks of casting lots (a completely random event) and says, "The lot is cast into the lap, but its every decision is from the LORD." Lest we think that our own efforts direct our lives, the psalmist declares, "For exaltation comes neither from the east nor from the west nor from the south. But God is the Judge: He puts down one, and exalts another."[2] God is our sovereign Lord, and it is according to His own secret council that some are raised up and some brought low.

God Reigns over Nature

We may speak of general providence as an overall principle, but I assert that particular events are all evidence of God's special providence, including so-called "natural" events. Even though such occurrences are governed by general laws which God has set over them, He still causes each individual occurrence. In the wilderness, God sent the south wind to bring His people a supply of quail, and God stirred up the storm which distressed Jonah's companions so that they threw him into the sea.[3] Some people argue with me on this point, claiming that these events were special and that God does not *normally* control the wind. However, I do not know how they explain Psalm 104: "He lays the beams of His upper chambers in the waters, who makes the clouds His chariot, who walks on the wings of the wind," or Psalm 107: "For He commands and raises the stormy wind, which lifts up the waves of the sea."[4]

It is not only storms and winds over which God claims sovereign power. We can all agree that conception of children follows certain natural laws, and yet God

---

[1] Proverbs 16:1

[2] Psalm 75:6-7

[3] Exodus 16:13, Jonah 1:4

[4] Psalm 104:3, Psalm 107:25

declares that the fruit of the womb is His reward. Thus, when Rachel demanded that Jacob give her a child, he replied angrily, "Am I in the place of God, who has withheld from you the fruit of the womb?"[1]

Finally, nothing is more common and ordinary than the production of bread, and yet God declares His authority over that as well. He threatens to take away from Jerusalem and Judah "the stock and the store, the whole supply of bread and the whole supply of water."[2] Indeed, what would be the point of praying for daily bread (as we do in the Lord's prayer) if our heavenly Father did not supply us with bread? A psalm even reminds us that the Lord "gives food to all flesh."[3]

Therefore, when we read in the Bible that God hears the cry of the righteous and that He is against the wicked, let us be comforted in the knowledge that all His creatures in heaven and on earth are His tools through which He accomplishes His purposes. We conclude that God not only rules over the earth by general providence in the laws of nature, but He also has a special purpose for everything.

Providence or Fate?

People who shun the doctrine of providence often accuse us of believing in fate. The same accusation was leveled against Augustine. Normally, I do not wish to get involved in big arguments over terminology, but in this case, I reject the word "fate" because it is an inappropriate description of our doctrine. That accusation is merely a shallow attempt to turn others against us by sticking a negative label on biblical truth.

Our belief in providence is not remotely similar to the pagan belief in fate. We are not Stoics; we do not attribute events to a chain of causes occurring by necessity in nature. We trust in the Lord, our Provider and King. From the very beginning of time, according to His wisdom, He has decreed what He will do, and now He carries out His decrees by His divine power.

We further believe that His providence governs not only nature but also the plans and desires of mankind.

---

[1] Genesis 30:2

[2] Isaiah 3:1

[3] Psalm 136:25

> **Remember!**
>
> Stoicism was a philosophy which taught that a divine force infuses everything in the universe.
>
> Stoics also believed that all events were predetermined by a long series of cause-and-effect relationships. Hence, Stoics had a fatalistic outlook on life.

You ask, "Does nothing at all happen by chance?" I reply (as Basil the Great also said) that "fortune" and "chance" are heathen words. Christians should not use such terms. If all success comes from God (and all trials also) then where is the place for luck?

Augustine wrote, "I regret that I have used the word 'fortune' in my writings against the academics. I never intended a reference to a goddess, but rather some chance happening, either good or bad … I made an effort to note when I mentioned 'fortune' that I was not using it in the common way because I know that a hidden order lies behind it. Events which appear random to us are merely the workings of a plan which we do not understand. Even though I clarified this in my writing, I still regret mentioning 'fortune' at all. I hear many people around me saying, 'So Fortuna pleased,' instead of saying (as they should), 'So God pleased.'"[1]

Augustine explains in many of his works that we cannot believe anything is left to chance unless we ultimately conclude that the whole universe moves randomly. Scholars often interpret Augustine wrongly when he declares that all things occur partly by the free will of man and partly by the providence of God.[2]

"I'll Take 'Obscure Church Fathers' for $700, Alex!"

Basil of Caesarea (330 AD – 379 AD), also called **Basil the Great**, is known both for his theological works and his interest in caring for the poor. He was bishop of Caesarea Mazaca in Cappadocia.

Basil promoted a monastic life of community, prayer, and hard work. Theologically, he is best known for his defense of Trinitarian doctrine against Arian heresy.

Mythology Corner

Fortuna was the Roman goddess of good luck. She was often depicted with a wheel, symbolizing the continual changes in life. Fortuna was considered to be a fickle goddess, sometimes even visiting bad luck upon the righteous and favor on the wicked for no reason.

Augustine took a stand against the worship of Fortuna in *City of God*. He dismissed her as a false deity and asked why anyone would even honor a supposed goddess who had so little discernment.

The true intention of Augustine's statement becomes abundantly clear when it is read in context. Augustine proceeds immediately to say that mankind is ruled by God's providence and that nothing can be done unless God ordains it. In his other works, he proves that the will of God is the ultimate cause of all things. Augustine never presents God as a distant deity gazing down on mankind from a watchtower. He declares that God's will is active, that it is the source of everything that happens.

---

[1] Augustine, *Retractions*, Book I, Chapter 1
[2] Augustine, *De Diversis Quaestionibus*

God's Hidden Plan

Even though nothing happens by chance, events often appear random because the reasons behind these events are hidden from us. Even though God has His purposes, these purposes are not obvious to us, and so it may appear that things occur by chance.

Suppose a man is traveling with trustworthy friends, but he wanders off and becomes lost. Confused, he blunders into a camp of thieves who murder him. This may appear to us as if it were a sad case of simple bad luck. However, in such an example, the man's death had already been decreed by God. The book of Job declares: "Since his days are determined, the number of his months is with You; You have appointed his limits, so that he cannot pass."[1]

How should a Christian feel when facing this sort of situation? Believers should treat these events as random in regard to nature, while also remembering that God rules over so-called "random events" by His divine providence. The same principle applies to future events. We must, of course, act as though the future is uncertain, since it is uncertain to us. We do not know God's plan, and so we behave as though things could go one way or another. Even so, our hearts should hold on to the certainty that nothing will ever take God by surprise.

---

[1] Job 14:5

CHAPTER 17
HUMAN RESPONSIBILITY

Reverence for God

The human mind has an unfortunate tendency to indulge in useless arguments. When people do not properly understand the doctrine of providence, this inclination is multiplied a hundredfold. Even people who claim to understand providence often do not apply it properly, and so, at this point, I believe it would be most beneficial to briefly discuss the applications of the doctrine of providence in the life of a believer. I will cover three topics: (1) the providence of God in reference to the past and future, (2) the means by which God carries out His plan, and (3) God's concern for mankind, especially the church.

Before I begin this discussion, I would like to make one more point. The reasons behind particular events in God's eternal plan are often hidden from us. Our minds may whisper doubts concerning God's love for us. We may wonder whether we are being flung about by blind fortune. We may even question whether God is amusing Himself by tossing people around like balls. If our minds were quiet and prepared to learn, we would realize that God's plan is far above our mundane ideas of how life should proceed. He has purposes higher than ours. He may be training His children to be patient, correcting them, teaching them self-control, or waking them from spiritual slumber. On the other hand, He may be casting down the arrogant and defeating the evil schemes of the wicked. Even when we cannot see the purpose of God's work, we should trust that God has His reasons. We must proclaim with David, "Many, O LORD my God, are Your wonderful works which You have done; and Your thoughts toward us cannot be recounted to You in order; if I would declare and speak of them, they are more than can be numbered."[1]

When difficulties arise, we would do well to consider whether our sin has brought punishment from God upon us (for we all need to repent often), but we cannot assume that bad circumstances *always* indicate that we are being punished

---

[1] Psalm 40:5

for sin. Consider how Christ responded to the question about the man born blind: "Neither this man nor his parents sinned, but that the works of God should be revealed in him."[1]

Our understanding is so limited. When we see someone afflicted by a disease which began even before birth, we tend to cry out that God is unmerciful, that He sends trouble on people who do not deserve it. However, Christ declares that if our eyes were clear we would see the glory of God shining even in those difficult situations.

We must be humble before God. It is not our place to demand that God answer to us and provide us with reasons for everything He does. We must learn to accept His will as a sufficient reason. Sometimes the sky is overshadowed with dark clouds, thunder rumbles, and terror overwhelms us. We may feel as though everything around us has been thrown into chaos. We look up to heaven for help, and all is quiet, as if God is unconcerned about our problems. These are precisely the moments in which we must remember that distress impairs our judgment. God is not far away. His wisdom is far greater than ours. He will keep everything under control and bring it all to its proper conclusion, according to His eternal plan.

We should never presume to pronounce judgment on God's plan. These are things which we cannot possibly understand, and we should remember that. People often angrily say, "I wish others would not be so hasty in judging me! They do not know what they are talking about!" And yet, these same people rush to blame God when they do not understand His plan and could not possibly know what they are talking about.

> ### O man, who are you to reply against God?
>
> Calvin emphasizes faith and humble acceptance of God's providence. He acknowledges that event may appear random, but he insists that this is only because we do not understand God's plan. He encourages his readers to remember even in great difficulty that God is not distant or uncaring. Faith requires that we trust God even in trials, and humility demands that we accept His decree without murmuring against Him.
>
> It is human nature to seek for a purpose behind our difficulties, and yet sometimes the reasons are hidden from us. Calvin declares that there is one simple reason which should always satisfy us: *This is God's will.* It is not for us to judge God's plans.

No one will properly understand God's providence except those who constantly bear in mind that they are dealing with their Maker. We must be reverent and humble. These days, so many bad teachers attack the doctrine of providence, refusing to admit that God has any greater power than they would like Him to have.

---

[1] John 9:3

They viciously assail us with vague accusations, as if we dreamed up this whole doctrine. They claim that the term "God's will" applies only to His commands and that there is no mystery to it. Evidence of God's sovereign providence is everywhere in Scripture, but they ignore it because it does not suit their philosophy. They dare not sling insults against God, and so they pick fights with us. I do not know how they explain verses such as Romans 11:33-34: "Oh, the depth of the riches both of the wisdom and knowledge of God! How unsearchable are His judgments and His ways past finding out! For who has known the mind of the LORD? Or who has become His counselor?"

Moses spoke beautifully about God's eternal plan: "The secret things belong to the LORD our God, but those things which are revealed belong to us and to our children forever, that we may do all the words of this law."[1] Moses urges us to remember God's law and also to reverently meditate upon His secret providence.

Therefore, since God proclaims Himself as the true King of the universe (which we are not), let us remember to be humble and respectful, submitting to His authority in all things, even those things which we do not understand.

Human Responsibility

Some vulgar characters have been blustering in their foolishness, claiming that there is no point in being cautious in life if God has already set the day on which each person will die. Reasonable people who wish to avoid danger will sometimes avoid a perilous road, or consult a doctor during an illness, or eat healthy food, or worry about poor construction in a house. But these scoundrels rebuke all reasonable people for their caution. These same troublemakers also claim that prayer is useless because God has already decided what people should receive. They make no plans for the future, because they say this would be tantamount to a declaration of war against God's providence. If a sin is committed, they declare that it is the will of God and that no one else is to blame!

There is no scriptural basis for this. The Bible easily reconciles human planning with God's providence. Solomon said, "A man's heart plans his way, but the LORD directs his steps."[2] God's eternal decrees do not prevent us in any way from planning for the future or organizing our lives, although our plans are always subject to His will. Obviously, God has set the boundaries of our lives, and

---

[1] Deuteronomy 29:29

[2] Proverbs 16:9

That Swine Quintin

The "vulgar characters" mentioned by Calvin in this chapter are again the **Libertines**. This heretical sect claimed that safety precautions were useless because God had already predestined the day of everyone's death. While this was disturbing enough, their teachings concerning sin were far worse. Calvin was enraged to hear them urging others to sin freely. They reasoned that God uses evil for His own good purposes, and so sin would ultimately glorify God.

The leader of the Libertine sect was **Quintin of Hainaut**, a tailor who began to pass himself off as a scholar in the court of a naïve lady named Marguerite. Calvin despised him, calling him "that swine Quintin," and exclaiming, "What has transformed Quintin and his tailor-companion into scholars has been their desire to be fed at ease and the fact that work does not agree with them."

Calvin considered the Libertine view of crime to be absolute stupidity. The Libertines taught that no criminal should be punished, because crime merely carried out the just purposes of God. Calvin noted that they would scoff at the misfortunes of others, but as soon as they suffered a trial of their own, they would forget all their fancy philosophy and fly into a rage.

In his treatise against the Libertines, Calvin tells of a humorous incident between a merchant named Etienne de la Forge (a personal friend of Calvin) and a Libertine cobbler. When the merchant was robbed, the cobbler told him that it would be wrong to seek justice or even to consider the theft an evil deed, because God had predestined it.

A few days later, the cobbler was also robbed. He instantly began to search frantically for the man who had stolen his money. Finally, he stopped at the house of Etienne de la Forge to bewail his terrible misfortune. The merchant asked him why he was discontent when God had predestined that he should be robbed.

Calvin concludes the story: "The poor man being confounded by his own words which he had used [earlier], went away completely crestfallen, his tail between his legs, and at the same time unreformed by it."[1]

yet He permits us to look after ourselves and our own safety. He has even warned us of potential dangers and given us the means of protecting ourselves. It is our duty to use those means which He has provided.

The imprudent say that a danger will not kill us unless God wills it, and that if God wills it, there is no avoiding death. For this reason, they exercise no caution at all. But what if the danger does not kill us *because* God has given us a way to overcome it? How could we defend failing to heed God when He warns us to take care lest we die? These foolish people refuse to admit what is obvious to everyone else: God has provided us with wisdom and good counsel in order to preserve our lives.

---

[1] Calvin, John. *Treatises Against the Anabaptists and Against the Libertines,* Trans. by Benjamin Wirt Farley. 1982. Baker Book House.

These same rash people claim that crime should not be punished, since it all happens within the providence of God. They say that theft, adultery, murder, and other serious sins are all predestined by God, and therefore, no one can be blamed for these things. They ask, "If God is chastising someone by allowing a thief to rob his house, then why should you punish the thief? He is carrying out the vengeance of God! And why would you condemn a murderer? He merely ended a life that God had already determined should end. If everyone is carrying out God's plan, why should we blame anyone for anything they do?"

I firmly deny that these miscreants are serving God in the manner that they claim. We should never imagine that we are serving the Lord when we act out our own wicked desires. We are required to obey God. Our efforts to carry out His will should always conform to His Word. Anything else is rebellion. It is true that no one can ultimately do anything outside God's plan. However, we should not be so foolish that we ramble along with no consideration for His commandments, intentionally breaking His law. God is infinitely wise and powerful, and He can use even evil to accomplish His good purposes. Yes, thieves, murderers, and other wicked people are still tools of God's providence, and the Lord uses them to carry out His plans. But this is no excuse! These profane people try to drag God down into sin and blame Him so that they will be excused, but it will not work! Their sin is like a dead body set out in the sun. As the sun beats down on it, it begins to stink. The warm rays of the sun may be causing the body to decompose, but no one would claim that the sun stinks. So also, when the stench of sin rises, no one should say that God is sinning.

These arrogant people are like dogs; they can only bark at God's justice from very far away. They cannot touch it.

The Comfort of Believers

The crazy rambling of these distracted people may be easily put aside when we consider the true meaning of providence. The heart of a believer knows that everything happens according to God's eternal plan and that nothing happens randomly (yet also allows for secondary causes, as the case may be). Christians may be confident that God watches over His children, and that nothing will happen except that which is ultimately for their good and their salvation. We know that God cares for His people first, and then for all His other creatures. There is nothing outside His control. As for mankind, their plans, desires, and abilities are subject to God, and He turns them this way and that way as He pleases.

The Bible is replete with promises assuring believers that God's providence is for their welfare: "Cast your burden on the LORD, and He shall sustain you; He shall never permit the righteous to be moved," and "He who dwells in the secret place of the Most High shall abide under the shadow of the Almighty," and "Can a woman forget her nursing child, and not have compassion on the son of her womb? Surely they may forget, yet I will not forget you."[1]

Since we reject the teachings of those who imagine that God is distant and uncaring, let us remember and be comforted by His mercy toward us. When Christ observed that not even a little sparrow falls to the ground without the will of the Father, He immediately applied the lesson to us, pointing out that we are of far greater worth than little birds and should never doubt God's tender care. He even added that the hairs of our head are counted by God.[2] What more could we ask? Not even a hair can fall from our heads outside of His will. He provides for all mankind, and especially for His church.

When trouble comes to us, we should immediately turn our hearts to God. The Lord gives us patience and peace of mind. If Joseph had spent all his time thinking about how his brothers had betrayed him, he would never have been able to demonstrate brotherly love toward them. He turned his thoughts to God, putting aside his anguish over the injustice done to him. He even comforted his brothers: "But now, do not therefore be grieved or angry with yourselves because you sold me here; for God sent me before you to preserve life."[3]

If Job had fixed his mind on thoughts of revenge against the Chaldeans, he would not have recognized it as the Lord's work. But, with his mind on God, he was able to proclaim in wonderful faith, "The LORD gave, and the LORD has taken away; blessed be the name of the LORD."[4]

When Shimei cursed and threw stones at David, the king might have focused on him and forgotten God. If David had done so, he would have wanted to strike out at Shimei. But David knew that Shimei was acting within the will of God, and so he responded, "Let him alone, and let him curse; for so the LORD has ordered him."[5]

---

[1] Psalm 55:22, Psalm 91:1, Isaiah 49:15

[2] Matthew 10:30-31

[3] Genesis 45:5

[4] Job 1:21

[5] II Samuel 16:11

Meditation on God's providence is the best medicine for anger and impatience. People who trust in the providence of God always know that God has ordained their trials, and that whatever God ordains will ultimately benefit His children. Whenever we are treated badly by others, let us overlook their insults. There is no point in dwelling on hurts; it only makes the injury more painful. It also gives us an unhealthy thirst for revenge. Instead, let us remember that whatever our enemy did to us was ultimately within the plan of God. God is always just.

Secondary Causes

> **Common Sense Calvinism**
>
> Calvin urges an industrious and sensible approach to life. He advises his readers to consider **secondary causes**. While God's providence rules over everyone and everything, we cannot use this as an excuse to sit around and do nothing. God gives us wisdom to make good decisions. He provides us with friends and family. He gives us work. These are all means through which He accomplishes His purposes, and so we should not neglect them.

Although we should remember that God is the source of everything (good and bad) that comes our way, we should not forget that there are also secondary causes. If someone is kind to us, should we neglect to thank them merely because the good deed was within God's plan? Of course not! We should demonstrate sincere gratitude and profusely thank those who have helped us. We should also give thanks to God, because He is the Provider of all good things, but it is not wrong to recognize people as ministers of God's compassion. It is also good to remember that it is by God's design that we find ourselves indebted to the service of others, and we should make every effort to repay kindnesses.

If a believer loses money or property because he was neglecting his duty or because he was involved in some foolish scheme, he should not merely chalk it up to the will of God. He should consider his own fault in the matter. If it is his responsibility to care for a sick person and he neglects his obligation so that the person dies, then he should acknowledge his failure to fulfill his duty. If deliberate wickedness produces some calamity, then there is no excuse, and such a thing should never be blamed on providence.

We should be especially mindful of secondary causes while planning for the future. We are blessed by God when we have good friends. We should never be hesitant to ask advice or to ask for help from those who are able to provide it. These are legitimate means by which God blesses and sustains us. Since no one knows exactly what the outcome of any particular course of action will be, we should work hard in whichever direction seems wise and helpful to our situation. Yet we must be careful that zeal for our preferred course of action does not blind us to the wisdom of God.

While friends are a great blessing, we should not place so much confidence in them that we become anxious when we must stand alone. Our minds should be fixed on the providence of God for our security. No circumstance should ever cause us to lose faith in God. Remember that Joab acknowledged that the outcome of the battle was in the hands of God, but he did not sit passively and wait for God to act. He rose up to fulfill his calling: "Be of good courage, and let us be strong for our people and for the cities of our God. And may the LORD do what is good in His sight."[1]

As we understand God's providence, we find that same conviction in our own hearts. We shy away from rashness and false confidence. We turn more often to God in prayer, while also filling our minds with hope and the knowledge of God's goodness to us. So we are able to stand secure against all the dangers which surround us.

Trust in the Lord

In human life, danger is everywhere and death is always lurking just around the corner. Sometimes death is not even that far away, considering that the human body can host innumerable diseases. A man cannot even move without carrying destruction along with him. Life is entangled with death. Whichever way you turn, there are things which can hurt you. People may die of heat, and they may also die of cold. Nothing is completely safe. If you board a ship, you are only inches from drowning. If you ride a horse, the animal may stumble and throw you off. If you walk along the street, a tile falling from a roof may hit you in the head. If you hide inside a walled garden, a snake may bite you. If you seal yourself inside your house, it may burn down. Crops may be destroyed by hail, disease, and drought. As terrifying as this list might be, it does not even mention such crimes as poison, treachery, and robbery which may occur at home or on the road.

Amid all these dangers, mankind must be miserable and terrified. Without some kind of help, we would be living (if you can call it living) every day as if a sword were always hanging over our necks. If our lives were governed by chance, we could never feel secure for a moment.

When the light of God's providence dawns in the soul of a believer, he is set free, not only from general day-to-day anxiety, but from *every* fear. Christians put

---

[1] II Samuel 10:12

their trust in their heavenly Father, and so they are comforted, because God rules over everything. He governs the world and everything in it according to His infinite wisdom, and nothing can happen except those things which He has appointed. Christians believe that God is with them and that He has commanded the angels to watch over them. God's children are confident, exclaiming, "The LORD is on my side; I will not fear. What can man do to me?"

---

[1] Psalm 118:6

CHAPTER 18
THE SOVEREIGNTY OF GOD

God's Will among Mankind

Solomon said, "The king's heart is in the hand of the LORD, like the rivers of water; He turns it wherever He wishes."[1] To phrase it another way, every thought is directed by the secret prompting of God.

Unless we understand that God works in this way, the Bible will make very little sense to us. The Scripture says several times that people became frightened when God filled their hearts with terror.[2] David was able to leave Saul's camp without anyone knowing because God cause them to sleep.[3] Over and over, we see God send sleep upon people, turn them over to madness, or harden their hearts. Most famously, Pharaoh's heart was hardened by God so that he continually resisted all the warnings of Moses. The Bible does not say that God merely gave Pharaoh permission to rebel, but rather that God *caused* the hardening Pharaoh's heart.[4] Moreover, this is not the only passage of Scripture in which we read of God hardening hearts. The book of Joshua tells us that God hardened the hearts of the Canaanites so that they waged war against the people of Israel.[5] Isaiah the prophet warned the Israelites that God would send the Assyrians against them with a command to plunder and destroy.[6] Obviously, God was not saying that He was going to add an 11th Commandment to teach us all to plunder and destroy. The Assyrians did not know God's law, nor were they obeying it. God prompted the Assyrians *internally* to carry out His judgment against Israel.

---

[1] Proverbs 21:1

[2] Leviticus 26:36

[3] I Samuel 26:12

[4] Exodus 9:12

[5] Joshua 11:30

[6] Isaiah 10:6

God often employs Satan to prompt the wicked to act wickedly. Satan performs his part of God's plan exactly as God has decreed and only so far as God has permitted. Scripture tells us that the evil spirit which tormented Saul came from the Lord, suggesting that it was a punishment from God.[1] The Bible also tells us that Satan blinds the minds of those who do not believe.[2] Paul tells us that God causes those who refuse to obey the truth to believe a lie.[3] He confirms this again in another epistle, stating that God gave people over to a debased mind.[4]

God is Not Sinful

God rules over the wicked, even their plans and desires. Does this mean that He is the Author of sin? If God is sovereign over the wicked, are evildoers unfairly condemned? Some would say that no one can be blamed for sin except God. Their misperception confuses God's will (His overall plan) with God's commandments. It is obvious from many examples in Scripture that there is a big difference between these two concepts. When Absalom defiled his father's concubines, this evil act punished David for his adultery, and yet it was still a shameful act.[5] When Shimei cursed David, David accepted it as chastisement from God, and yet Shimei was not keeping God's law as found in Scripture.[6]

We must understand that, although God accomplishes His purposes through the wicked according to His hidden will, they are not excused for their sin. It is not as if they were obeying the Ten Commandments. No, they are in rebellion against the precepts of God.

Let us examine the story in I Kings 12 which tells of the ascension of Jeroboam to the throne. The people rejected the government provided by God when they rebelled against the house of David. Even so, we know that it was the will of God for Jeroboam to be anointed king. Through the prophet Hosea, God first complains that people set up the king against His ordinance, a king which God Himself did not acknowledge. However, God later speaks through Hosea again to say that He gave them a king in His anger.[7] How do we reconcile these two verses?

---

[1] I Samuel 16:14

[2] II Corinthians 4:4

[3] II Thessalonians 2:11

[4] Romans 1:28-29

[5] II Samuel 16:22

[6] II Samuel 16:10-11

[7] Hosea 8:4, Hosea 13:11

Jesus and Judas: A Study in the Sovereignty of God

In his final chapter of Book I, Calvin grapples with the question of God's role in evil. Calvin confirms that God uses evil for His good purposes. The obvious question arises: if God causes bad things to happen, then is God evil? Calvin responds with a resounding "No!"

To illustrate his point, he quotes Augustine's commentary on the betrayal of Christ. The Bible declares that God gave His Son to die for us. The Bible also tells us that Christ gave Himself as a sacrifice for us. Finally, we are told that Judas betrayed Christ to His death. Out of all these, only Judas sinned. Considering that their actions produced the same result (the death of Jesus), why is only Judas blamed?

The answer has to do with motives. God gave His Son to save us. Christ died for us to redeem us. Judas was greedy for money.

There are many examples of this concept in everyday life. Suppose a man pushes his young son out of the path of an oncoming car. The child may be confused and frightened, wondering why his father suddenly struck out at him. The child only blames his father, however, because he does not understand the reason. The father was not being cruel; he was saving his son. Motives can determine culpability for an action.

Calvin explains that God has higher purposes which we do not understand. Even when we receive difficult trials from His hand, we must trust that He has sent these things for our eternal good.

The answer is obviously that the people who revolted against the house of David were in rebellion against God's divine order, and yet God ordained that this would happen in order to punish Solomon for his unfaithfulness. God does not desire disobedience, and yet, with other purposes in mind, His justice compels it.

I hope that my readers will consider these things carefully. For those humble in spirit, the explanation of Augustine will suffice: "The Father delivered up the Son to death. Christ delivered up His body to death. Judas delivered up his Lord to death. With all of this delivering up, why do we consider God just and man guilty? It is because God and man did not have the same reason for doing it."[1]

Judas' betrayal of Christ did not become sinless simply because God Himself had willed that Jesus would die on the cross for our sins. There is no more reason to suppose that Judas' sin was the fault of God then there would be to suppose that our salvation should be credited to Judas.

If some people think that my teaching on this matter is too harsh, I am comfortable with that, because I am merely repeating the doctrine found in Scripture. I would be very uncomfortable indeed if I were instead refusing to accept

---

[1] Augustine, *Letters*, Chapter 2.

the Bible's instruction. If God did not wish us to speak of such things, He would not have taught them to the prophets and apostles with the command to preach them. Wisdom requires that we be humble and teachable before holy Scripture. As for those who continue to scoff, even after it is clear that they are actually scoffing at the Word of God, I see no point in making any further effort to persuade them.

INDEX